Berner Beiträge zur Nationalökonomie   Band 71

Herausgegeben von
E. Baltensperger, R. E. Leu, G. Stephan
o. Professoren an der Universität Bern

Tobias F. Rötheli

Monetary Regimes, Risk, and International Capital Accumulation

Verlag Paul Haupt Bern · Stuttgart · Wien

Tobias F. Rötheli (1958) holds a doctorate in economics of the University of Bern. He has worked at the Swiss National Bank and has been a visiting Scholar at the Federal Reserve Bank of St. Louis, Harvard University, and Stanford University. Presently, he is a lecturer in Economics at the University of Bern.

Die Deutsche Bibliothek – CIP-Einheitsaufnahme

Rötheli, Tobias F.:
Monetary regimes, risk, and international capital accumulation /
Tobias F. Rötheli. –
Bern ; Stuttgart ; Wien : Haupt, 1995
(Berner Beiträge zur Nationalökonomie ; Bd. 71)
Zugl.: Bern, Univ., Habil-Schr., 1994
ISBN 3-258-05258-1
NE: GT

Alle Rechte vorbehalten
Copyright © 1995 by Paul Haupt Berne
Jede Art der Vervielfältigung ohne Genehmigung des Verlages ist unzulässig
Dieses Papier ist umweltverträglich, weil chlorfrei hergestellt
Printed in Switzerland

To my parents

Contents

Preface	ix

Chapter 1 Introduction and Summary	1
1.1 A Survey of the Chapters	1
1.2 Policy Conclusions	4
1.3 The Wider Context of this Book	5

Chapter 2 Inflation Risk and International Capital Accumulation	7
2.1 Features of the Model	10
2.2 Monetary Regimes	22
2.3 Solutions	29
2.4 Conclusions	34
Appendix 2.A: Closed Form Solutions for the Quadratic Case	35
Appendix 2.B: Portfolio Variance under Different Monetary Regimes	37

Chapter 3 Exchange Rate Risk and International Capital Allocation	39
3.1 The Individual's Choice	40
3.2 Macroeconomic Equilibrium	46
3.3 The Effect of Floating the Exchange Rate	52
3.4 The Feldstein-Horioka Puzzle	58
3.5 Exchange Rate Regime and the Net Foreign Asset Position	59
3.6 Considerations of Efficiency and Political Economy	61
3.7 Conclusions	66
Appendix 3.A: Derivation of the Mean-Variance Utility Function	67
Appendix 3.B: The Effect of Unequal β-Parameters	68

Chapter 4 **An Empirical Investigation on Exchange Rate Regimes and Capital Accumulation: Switzerland 1950 - 1990**   71

4.1 The Historical Background	73
4.2 Estimating the Effect on Capital Accumulation	75
4.3 Conclusions	80
Appendix 4: Data and Sources	81

Chapter 5 **The Effects of Variable Inflation on the Capital Stock and Consumption**   83

5.1 Steady Inflation	84
5.2 Variable Inflation	88
5.3 Conclusions	93

References   95

Index   101

Preface

One line of thought concerning monetary policy addresses questions of how to operate within a given regime, that is, within a given system of rules and procedures. Questions which can be pursued along these lines concern the quantification of the rules and the choice of actions necessary to achieve the stated targets. An alternative way of thinking about monetary policy is to think about what type of monetary regime a central bank should choose. Is money stock targeting superior to interest rate targeting, is a combination of the two even better, or should a country simply fix its exchange rate? It is my impression that thinking within central banks tends to be more centered on questions regarding the operation of a particular regime while the comparison of regimes is more academics' work. This does not only reflect a division of labor, I believe, but tells something about the perceived practical importance of research findings. Historically, changes in monetary regimes often only happen as a response to crises. The system of fixed exchange rates of Bretton Woods, as an example, was abandoned because the magnitude of internationally transmitted inflation exceeded a level many member nations were prepared to bear. For countries like Switzerland there was just no answer to the problem of inflation within the regime existing at the time. Still, regime comparisons remain important. Decision makers who are forced into a regime switch are likely to make better choices when they have a clear notion of the consequences the alternatives might entail.

The present book is a contribution to the evaluation of monetary regimes. Its basic focus of research was set in 1989 when I was an economist with the Swiss National Bank. A grant from the Swiss National Science Foundation enabled me to spend three years in the United States. Most of the material incorporated in this book was written while I was a visiting scholar at Harvard University and at Stanford University. I wish to thank Robert Barro and John Taylor for sponsoring my stay at these two fine institutions. Jürg Niehans has contributed excellent comments on various versions of my manuscript and has helped clarify many issues. I am also much indebted to Ernst Baltensperger and Peter Kugler of the University of Bern who have supported this project from its very beginning. They acted as referees when the results of my research were submitted as a Thesis of Habilitation at the University of Bern. Chapters 3 and 4 were presented at the international economics seminar at Stanford University. I am grateful to Ronald McKinnon and Robert Staiger for that opportunity and their comments. A presentation at the Swiss National Bank resulted in improvements in chapter 4. Walter von Siebenthal and Mathias Zurlinden have helped in the last part of this project and their professional judgement is particularly valued. Ruth Parham has helped with many suggestions to improve the style of the text. Finally, I would like to thank the editors of this series for publishing my book.

1

Introduction and Summary

This study is concerned with the analysis of long-term effects of various monetary regimes. More specifically, we are interested in how monetary regimes influence the variability of inflation and exchange rates which in turn affects capital accumulation. The main theme pursued here is the effect of uncertainty concomitant with these variations. Risk-averse agents react to these risks both with their savings and by their portfolio allocation decisions. The question then is: how does the choice of monetary regime affect savings and the allocation of savings among countries? The effects of monetary regimes are analyzed in models that take individual maximization as point of departure. Their common theme is the focus on physical capital. Chapters 2, 3, and 4 deal with the effects of inflation risk and exchange rate risk on asset returns and, ultimately, capital accumulation. Chapter 5 deals with the effects of fully anticipated fluctuations - variations that do not induce any risk. This last chapter then draws attention to the fact that variability of the predictable part of inflation also matters. The following section surveys all the topics covered.

1.1 A Survey of the Chapters

Chapter 2 analyzes the effect of the choice of monetary regime on savings, capital accumulation, and welfare. The four regimes considered are money stock targeting, price level targeting, the one-sided currency peg, and the two-sided currency peg. In a model of two identical economies an ordering of these regimes with respect to their effect on investment and welfare is derived. The model assumes that purchasing power parity holds and thus does not address issues regarding real exchange rate variations. The focus is on inflation risk. The various monetary regimes differ in their effects because we assume the return on investment to be influenced by the inflation rate. The literature typically sees a negative correlation and explains this with the presence of a non-neutral tax system which decreases the after-tax return during inflation and increases it during deflation [see, e. g., Feldstein, Green, and Sheshinski (1978)]. In the circumstance described it turns out that the ordering of the monetary regimes with respect to their effect on investment is the following: Investment is highest under the regime of the one-sided exchange rate peg followed by the regime of money stock control, the two-sided peg and the regime of price level control. The ordering with respect to welfare (assessed by the level of expected utility attained) is the reverse of the above. This outcome reflects the fact that increased savings result from increased return uncertainty.

Chapter 3 describes a situation with deviations from purchasing power parity. It explores the notion that a regime of flexible exchange rates leads to larger fluctuations in real exchange rates than a regime of pegged currencies. In my view the models of chapters 2 and 3 complement each other. The line of divison - whether purchasing parity holds or not - serves as a simplifying device for the study of the various problems involved: chapter 2 studies the effects of inflation risk while chapter 3 investigates the role of exchange rate risk. Those who see merit in the proposition that purchasing power parity holds even in the short run may be more interested - from the perspective of monetary regime evaluation - in the results of chapter 2. For them chapter 3 is an investigation of the effect of exchange rate risk (caused by forces other than monetary policy) on capital allocation.

The model of chapter 3 also builds on the idea that investors are interested in diversifying their savings internationally. Investors in this two-country world can invest in domestic as well as foreign equities and bonds. Variations in the real exchange rate add risk to foreign investment. The model takes into account that investors have the choice - either by bond transactions or on the forward exchange market - to hedge their exchange rate risk. The results emerging from the analysis can be intuitively grasped when we consider, by way of an example, the effects of the transition from fixed to flexible exchange rates. For the capital market equilibrium it is crucial which country emerges as the one with the lower bond return following the move to flexible exchange rates. Given that the expected change in the real exchange rate is zero the interest rate differential corresponds to the foreign exchange risk premium which determines the cost of hedging foreign investments. The investor of the country with the negative interest rate differential after the transition to floating currencies has to pay a positive premium to hedge the exchange rate risk on his foreign investment and will, as a result, want to hold a larger portion of his wealth in domestic equities. For the investor of the other country equity investment across the border also becomes more interesting in this case. She will be able to engage in bond or forward exchange transactions that will hedge the currency risk on her investment abroad while also yielding a positive net return. Hence, equity investment in the low interest rate country becomes more attractive for all investors. As a result, the capital stock in that country rises with the transition from fixed to flexible exchange rates. It is the diminishing marginal product of capital that limits the inflow of capital into this country. Which country ends up in this situation depends on the physical investment opportunities, the wealth levels, the variance and the covariance of capital returns, the variance of the exchange rate, and the risk aversion of investors. The analysis in chapter 3 further suggests that part of the home bias of investment documented by Feldstein and Horioka (1980) is due to exchange rate risk. It is shown that, under a flexible exchange rate, a country's investment should be expected to rise by more than its proportion in the world capital stock when domestic savings rise.

Chapter 4 is an empirical investigation based on the results of chapter 3. It addresses the question of how the transition from fixed to flexible exchange rates affects capital accumulation in a small open economy. The country under investigation is Switzerland which has had two distinctly different monetary regimes in the post-war period. Until the early 1970s the Swiss pegged their currency to the dollar. In the period since then the Swiss National Bank has been pursuing a policy of money stock targeting geared to keeping inflation in check. Consistent with the theoretical results of chapter 3 it is found that Switzerland which - after the transition to flexible exchange rates - emerged with a positive foreign exchange risk premium, also experienced an increase in its physical capital stock.[1] This assessment is based on econometric estimates of investment equations. Hence, the data on Switzerland support the conjecture that a small wealthy country with relatively poor physical investment possibilities is likely to attract more capital under flexible exchange rates.

Since this text focuses on the role of fluctuations induced by monetary policy, chapter 5 addresses the question whether even fully anticipated fluctuations - variations that do not induce any risk - can have an effect on capital accumulation. It is shown in a monetary growth model with an infinite horizon

---

[1] See Frankel and MacArthur (1988) and Frankel (1991) for evidence on international interest rate differentials and currency risk premia.

4 *Monetary Regimes, Risk, and International Capital Accumulation*

that even when there is no uncertainty associated with changes in the inflation rate there will still be interesting effects of inflationary variability. It turns out that inflationary variability, induced by money supply variability, can raise or lower the capital stock depending, inter alia, on the average level of inflation. The practice of using ever more refined procedures to eliminate the predictable part of inflationary variations common in econometric studies dealing with the effect of inflationary variability on aggregate income is questioned by this result.

1.2 Policy Conclusions

This section summarizes several key findings relevant to economic policy that emerge from this book. The various models and the empirical investigation document that the choice of monetary regime does indeed affect capital accumulation and welfare of an economy. In this respect the widespread procedure of choosing and shaping a monetary regime merely based on the possibilities for stabilization policies that particular regime offers misses an important point. From the perspective of this book a simple guideline can be proposed to bring the point mentioned into the policy discussion: Choosing a monetary arrangement that reduces the variance of the return on savings is likely to generate welfare gains. The return on a country's savings is understood to be the return on its wealth including the foreign components of wealth. Hence, which regime is most beneficial to a country depends also on the regimes adopted by other economies. The economies that are of importance with respect to this question are the economies whose savings a country attracts and the economies whose investment possibilities attract the country's savings. Hence, it can turn out that fixed exchange rates, for example, are only advantageous when the countries involved in the exchange rate fixing collectively commit themselves to price level stabilization.[2]

As is the case with the international liberalization of trade, potential welfare gains have to be distributed over the different social groups - owners of capital and land and workers in the present context - of an economy in order to make a change of regime advantageous to all. However, the distributional problems of making welfare improving changes not only affect the citizens of a single country but also the dealings between countries. Since the

---

[2] See chapter 2.

choice of monetary regime affects the international allocation of capital it can be advantageous for a group of countries to coordinate their choices. The outcome of such a coordination can mean that capital flows to new destinations. If the output gains outweigh the output losses then everybody can potentially be made better off. As in the national sphere discussed before, transfer payments may become necessary to compensate the losers. Without such a transfer scheme wealthy economies with relatively scarce physical investment possibilities, like Switzerland, are likely to make different assessments than relatively poor countries undergoing industrialization and in need of foreign funds. Consider the entry into a fixed exchange rate zone as an example. In a rich country the reduction in exchange rate risk is likely to induce a capital outflow. Wage earners can forsee the impending decline of their incomes and will oppose the transition to fixed exchange rates. In a poor country, on the other hand, workers are likely to gain from such a transition.[3] It follows that for a rich country to join a fixed exchange rate system, even if potentially advantageous, is a politically more difficult move. This may help to explain why Switzerland has not tied its currency to a foreign currency again since the abandonment of the Bretton Woods system.[4]

To the degree that - under a given monetary regime - there is scope for decisions regarding the magnitude of variations in inflation, it should be reckoned that these variations, even when fully anticipated, can have consequences for savings and capital accumulation. It is, however, difficult to say whether a steadying of inflation in a country, given its monetary system and its average level of inflation, will raise or lower the level of consumption attainable. At this point the results presented in chapter 5 should only be taken to indicate that the amplitude of variations can matter even when people anticipate these variations correctly.

Chapters 2, 3, 4, and 5 provide a much more detailed discussion of policy implications than is possible here.

1.3 The Wider Context of this Book

The existing literature on monetary and exchange rate regimes covers many topics. The present work focuses on capital accumulation and does not

---

[3] See chapter 3.
[4] See chapter 4.

integrate many other issues of relevance to the choice of regime. Hence, it seems advisable to mention related themes that have received much attention in the literature. The contributions to the question of regime choice can be roughly divided into four groups: The first group centers around contributions by Mundell and Fleming. The basic question examined in their work is how the choice of an exchange rate regime affects the possible use of monetary and fiscal policies for Keynesian stabilization policies.[5] A second body of work deals with so-called optimum currency areas.[6] In this literature the main question is whether mobility of resources (especially labor mobility) between countries is substantial enough to avoid unemployment. If labor mobility is low flexible exchange rates are socially superior to fixed exchange rates. Changes in the nominal exchange rate are then socially less costly than changes in national price levels when changes in demand necessitate an adjustment of the real exchange rate.

A third tradition of analysis was initiated by Poole (1970). In his famous contribution Poole analyzes the shock-absorbing capacities of an interest rate and a money supply regime. Subsequent work has applied the same type of stochastic macromodel to the comparison between exchange rate regimes.[7] The optimal regime viewed from this perspective depends on the sources of the shocks hitting the economy as well as on their variances, and the covariances between them. This first type of stochastic models was complemented within a few years by a different type of models addressing issues of uncertainty: Lucas (1982) and Helpman and Razin (1982) represent this tradition of analysis in open-economy macroeconomics. This strand of the literature is firmly rooted in microeconomic analysis. Apart from the concept of individual maximization, these studies also assume continuous market clearing and nominal price flexibility. The present volume is most closely tied to this latter tradition.

---

[5] See Mundell (1960) and Fleming (1962) and also Niehans (1975).
[6] See Mundell (1961).
[7] See, e. g., Argi (1994).

2

Inflation Risk and International Capital Accumulation

The specific question the model in this chapter addresses is the following: how do different monetary regimes affect savings and the distribution of savings between domestic and foreign investment? The conceptual building blocks are individual maximization, market clearing, and nominal price flexibility. Early contributions with this orientation came from Lucas (1982) and Helpman and Razin (1982). The contributions in this tradition generally assume exogenous production. Hence, there is no capital in these models.[1] In the present model, however, physical capital takes center stage. The setup of the model is simple. We assume a world with two countries that have identical features. This means that the two countries are inhabited by an equal number of identical individuals and that the production possibilities are identical. This allows us to focus on the behavior of the representative individual. The agent optimizes his expected utility over two periods. The individual receives a fixed endowment in the first

---

[1] Lucas explains the reluctance to integrate production in these models with a problem pointed out by Grandmont and Younes (1973). According to these authors a monetary equilibrium with production based on a Clower constraint [see Clower (1967)] is generally not pareto-efficient. I don't see how this point would interfere with the analysis in this chapter. Recently, Aizenman (1992) presented a macroeconomic model in which the exchange rate regime influences aggregate investment. In his setup, multinational firms make direct investments and react in a risk-neutral way to the regime-dependent possibilities of diversifying production internationally. In the present model, in contrast, the accumulation of capital and its internationally diversified allocation is driven by risk aversion. Gertler and Grinols (1982) investigate another type of model in which the effect of inflation uncertainty on capital accumulation can be studied.

period and has to live on his savings in the second period.[2] This is the set-up familiar from the life-cycle model. Period one marks the (certain) present while period two marks the future which brings uncertain developments. The results suggested are not specific to the two-period frame chosen. Mirman (1971) has shown that the results of the type of problem analyzed here are equivalent to an infinite horizon problem. We assume that the same good is produced in the two countries. Hence, the relative price is always one and we cannot address fluctuations of the real exchange rate. Fluctuations of the real exchange rate and their effect on international portfolio diversification and capital allocation will be the central topic of chapter 3 of this book. The model in this chapter makes the case that the choice of monetary regime is likely to affect capital accumulation and welfare even when the condition of purchasing power parity holds. The model is inspired by Svensson's (1989) use of the state preference framework to handle uncertainty.[3] The state preference framework was pioneered by Arrow and Debreu and applied to investment theory by Hirshleifer three decades ago.[4]

The model draws on several empirical findings. There are basically four empirical pillars. They shall be detailed in turn and summarized in table 2.1. First, returns on capital are positively correlated with economic activity. Fama (1981), for example, shows strong positive correlations for the U. S. between changes in the rate of return on capital and changes in industrial production. Second, it has been documented repeatedly that output levels co-move internationally. Recently, Backus, Kehoe and Kydland (1993) have reported correlations between the output of nine OECD countries and the United States. All these correlations are positive and vary between 0.41 (for Italy) and 0.76 (for Canada). The correlation between U. S. output and an European aggregate is 0.66. Based on the two regularities reported it is not surprising that stock returns also co-move internationally. Kupiec (1991), for example, reports positive correlations between stock index returns of fifteen OECD countries. This is the third element that will be of importance in the model. The fourth regularity the model takes into account is the association of capital returns and

---

[2] This endowment can be thought of as labor income where labor is inelastically supplied and the wage does not depend on the capital stock. As indicated towards the end of section 2.3, non-zero endowments in the second period do not change the qualitative results proposed.

[3] Like the authors cited above, Svensson assumes exogenous production, that is, he does not include physical capital.

[4] See, e. g., Arrow (1971), Debreu (1959) and Hirshleifer (1965).

inflation. In the present model expected inflation is zero. Hence, we are concerned with the correlation between *unexpected* inflation and the stock return. Ammer (1994) reports regression results showing the effect of unexpected inflation changes on stock returns for ten countries. In eight countries considered (including the U. S., Germany, and Switzerland) the effect of inflation innovations on equity returns is negative. This confirms the findings of Fama and Schwert (1977) for the U. S.

The theory explaining this non-neutrality favored here is due to Feldstein, Green, and Sheshinski (1978). They explain the negative correlation with the presence of a non-neutral tax system. The tax theory framework implies the same sign of the correlation between stock returns and both expected and unexpected inflation. The second theory addressing the association between inflation and stock returns is due to Tobin (1958).[5] In the explanation outlined by Feldstein et al. two elements are of particular importance: First, when depreciation deductions for corporations are based on the nominal purchase price of assets an inflationary environment will tend to reduce real depreciations and lower corporate profits. Second, with a nominal capital gains tax inflation decreases the after-tax return during inflation and increases it during deflation.

Within the tax theory framework there is a possibility of a positive correlation between the after-tax return on investment and inflation. This can occur if the corporate tax structure permits an interest deduction that includes the inflation component.[6] Another case in which a positive correlation between inflation and capital return can result is when firms pay factors of production based on contracts that fix nominal wages and interest rates. In view of these possibilities we will, towards the end of section 2.3, also consider the case of a positive correlation between unexpected inflation and capital returns.

---

[5] In Tobin's view an increase in inflation means an increase in expected inflation and inflation uncertainty. Higher uncertainty raises the riskiness of assets which in turn raises the rate of return investors require of these assets. Higher inflation leading to a higher equilibrium return necessitates a decrease in the stock price which means a decline in the actual current return. This view is not detailed any further because in all cases studied here expected inflation is zero and the expected return is invariant to the monetary regime.

[6] See Driffill, Mizon, and Ulph (1990).

Table 2.1 Empirical Pillars of the Model

Correlation between	and	Sign of Correlation Coefficient
Stock Return	Economic Activity	Positive
Output Country i	Output Country j	Positive
Stock Return Country i	Stock Return Country j	Positive
Stock Return	Unexpected Inflation	Negative

2.1 Features of the Model

In the present framework individuals can invest in a capital good installed domestically and in a capital good installed in the foreign country. The return on these two possible projects is independent of the total amount of investment (i. e., we assume constant returns). The expected returns in the two locations are identical.[7] The state of either economy is described by two attributes: price level movement and business conditions. With business conditions we mean just the level of productivity of the economy. To keep things simple the attribute 'business conditions' takes only two values while the attribute 'price level movement' can take three values. For the attribute 'price level movement' we have inflation, a stable price level, or deflation. For the attribute 'business conditions' we have either a boom or a recession. Hence, we have six possible states or combinations of attributes in either country: boom/inflation,

---

[7] This is in accordance with the assumption of two identical economies. Besides this, it is of importance when we think of a situation in which the returns on the two projects are perfectly correlated. If the returns were not identical this would lead to a situation where all savings would go to the higher return country.

boom/stable price level, boom/deflation, recession/inflation, recession/stable price level, and recession/ deflation. With the two countries considered we potentially have 36 states of the world. We will see shortly how the differences in the monetary regimes can be shown in a matrix of the states of the world.

The return on investment varies with the state of the economy. This is one of the empirical regularities described before. As indicated, the attribute 'business conditions' is directly related to the productivity of investment. These stochastic fluctuations of the productivity are not explained in the model. The second determinant of the return on investment is the channel through which different monetary regimes affect savings and capital allocation. We model the return on investment (the interest rate) as moving inversely to the inflation rate. The focus on this link suggests that this non-neutrality is seen as a major channel through which monetary policy can affect capital formation. I neither model the transactions between the government and the private sector nor provide a technical account of how tax revenues are used.[8] However, one provision has to be made for the case where a nominal capital gains tax is the source of the effect of inflation on the capital return. In this case government revenues rise with inflation. If government revenues go partly into public investment these revenues may lead to further effects on private capital returns. In order to keep the stated direction of the effect of inflation on returns we rule out the case where public investment increases the productivity of private investment to such an extent that the primary effect of the capital gains tax is overcompensated. The present analysis, however, is not limited to the case of a negative correlation between inflation and capital returns. Section 2.3 discusses the results for the opposite case as well.

The inflation theory used here is the simplest possible: The quantity theory of money with a constant velocity of circulation holds. It is further assumed that central banks have full control over their money supply. It follows that, when the central bank of one of the countries increases its money supply by x%, with that country's aggregate production remaining constant, then the price level also increases by x%. Alternatively, an increase in output (i. e., an increase in money demand) with an unchanged money supply lowers the price level. By the same token, the price level can be stabilized in the light of an increase in aggregate production when the central bank increases its money supply proportionally to the increase in production. The three cases mentioned are shown in figure 2.1. The price level (P), the money supply (M),

---

[8] See Helpman (1981) and Helpman and Razin (1982) for details on these issues.

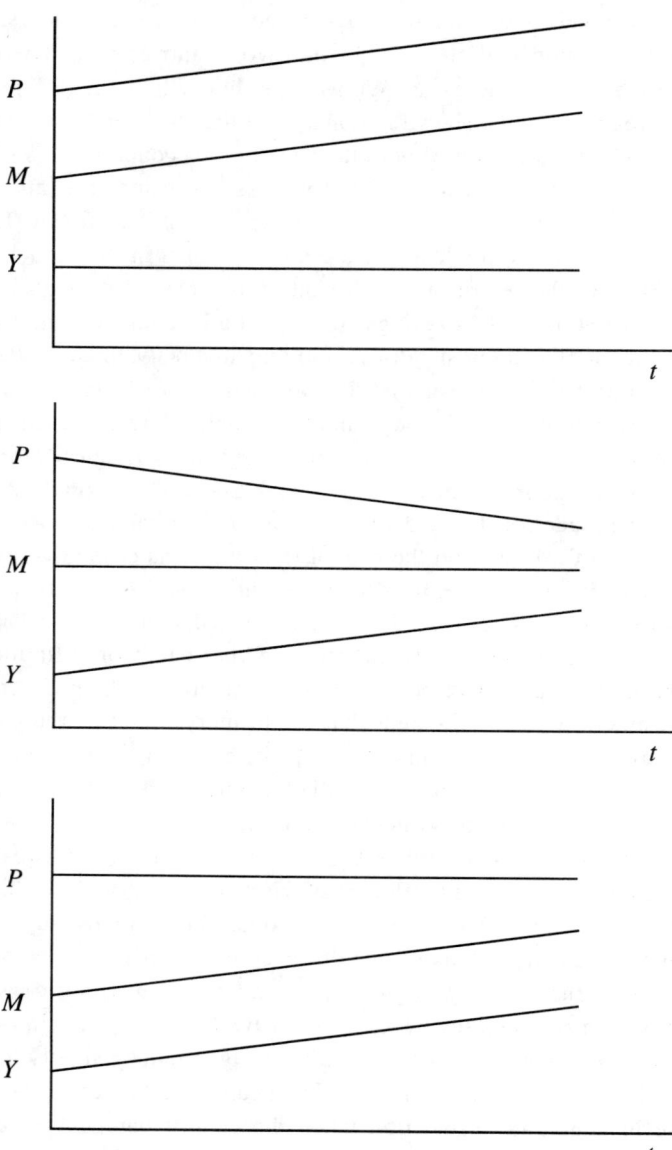

Figure 2.1 *Implications of the Quantity Theory*

and aggregate output (Y) are on the vertical axis (in logarithmic units) and time is on the horizontal axis. The top panel indicates the case where a constant level of total output is combined with an increase in the money supply: the result is an increase in the price level (i. e., inflation). The middle panel indicates the case where aggregate output, and hence money demand, increases but money supply remains unchanged: the result is a decrease in the price level (i. e., deflation). Finally, the bottom panel indicates the case where money supply moves proportionally to money demand: the result is a stable price level.

It has become customary in the macroeconomic literature to outline a microeconomic account for the regularities between the money supply, output, and the price level. Readers who are not interested in this exercise are invited to skip the next three paragraphs and resume reading shortly before equation (2.1) where we return to the decision problem of the individual. The simplest way to justify the quantity theory of money is by assuming that goods have to be purchased for money. Hence, every transaction involves a money transfer. The sequence of markets and transactions in a cash-in-advance economy is outlined in Stockman (1980), and a two-period version is dealt with in detail in an appendix to Svensson (1987). In the following I will give a short account of how the quantity theory emerges when one proceeds along these lines in my model.

From now on the two countries involved are termed land A and land B, respectively. The former is called the home country and the latter is called the foreign country. At the beginning of the first period the inhabitants of both countries get a money transfer in the currency of their country (M_1 and M^*_1, respectively, the asterisk indicating foreign variables). With this currency the individual in country A buys the goods for his first period consumption (c_1), the goods to be used for domestic investment (I^A) and the goods to be used for foreign investment (I^B). For the purchase of I^B the individual needs to buy foreign money. Because of symmetry, country A's demand for country B's goods is equal to country B's demand for country A's goods ($I^B = I^{*A}$). Hence, at the beginning of period one the domestic residents receive the foreign currency to buy I^B in exchange for the domestic currency which the foreign residents need to buy I^{*A}. The foreign currency necessary for the second period transaction is not acquired in a second-period spot market. Instead, similar to Lucas (1982), I allow the individuals to pool their monetary risk. The monetary risk in the present setting consists of the uncertainty regarding the amount of foreign exchange necessary in period two. When domestic residents and foreigners agree in advance to exchange half their respective money stocks, the monetary risk vanishes.

Since nobody wants to hold money from one period to the next in the presence of opportunity costs and the absence of monetary risk, all money is spent on the endowment (e and e^*).[9] When the entire domestic money stock is spent on the domestic endowment we have $M_1 = P_1 e$ and, correspondingly, the foreign money market equilibrium condition is $M^*_1 = P^*_1 e^*$. From this it immediately follows that $P_1 = M_1/e$ and $P^*_1 = M^*_1/e^*$. This means that the quantity theory holds in the first period.

At the end of the first period (the beginning of the second period) the individual gets the cash revenue from the sale of the first period income (the endowment). This revenue equals M_1 and M^*_1, respectively. In addition, each individual gets a new money transfer (positive or negative) that sets the money holdings to M_2 and M^*_2, respectively. At this point the state of the world in period two is revealed. Hence, the individuals learn about their second-period income. Since monetary pooling distributes the two monies equally among the residents of the two countries, the domestic country's inhabitant now spends $M_2/2$ to buy domestic goods $R_s^A I^A$ and $M^*_2/2$ to buy the foreign goods $R_s^B I^B$. Here, the symbols R_s^A and R_s^B refer to the capital returns in the two countries in various states (s) of the world. Similarly, the foreign country's inhabitant spends $M_2/2$ to buy $R_s^A I^{*A}$ and $M^*_2/2$ to buy $R_s^B I^{*B}$. The equilibrium conditions for the two money markets are therefore $M_2 = (R_s^A I^A + R_s^A I^{*A})P_2$ and $M^*_2 = (R_s^B I^B + R_s^B I^{*B})P^*_2$ or - written for the two equilibrium price levels - $P_2 = M_2/(R_s^A I^A + R_s^A I^{*A})$ and $P^*_2 = M^*_2/(R_s^B I^B + R_s^B I^{*B})$. Since the expressions in parentheses correspond to the second period production in the respective country, the quantity theory is also valid in that period.[10] With the one-good assumption, our two economies will have their exchange rate move according to purchasing power parity. This means that the exchange rate movement will be equal to the difference in the two inflation rates.

---

[9] The question arises: who holds the money between transaction periods? One obvious way to think about this is to assume that individuals own separate production entities. These firms sell their goods for money and later pay their dividends in money. In this framework the money stays in the firms most of the time.

[10] It remains to be said that at the end of the second period there will be revenue from the sale of the second period's income. It is typically assumed in the literature that this revenue is taxed away. The important point is that no use can be made of these cash revenues.

We now return to the decision problem of the individual. In order to simplify notation the endowment in the first period is set to one. The discount factor is denoted by ρ (where $1 > \rho > 0$). Hence, the maximization problem can be written in its general form as:

$$\text{Max } U(I^A, I^B) = u(1 - I^A - I^B) + \rho E u(R_s^A I^A + R_s^B I^B) \tag{2.1}$$

The effect of the state of the economy on the return on capital is parametrized in the following way. The effect of the state of business conditions is captured by the parameter β (where $\beta > 1$). In good times the capital productivity is β while in bad times it is one. Good times (booms) and bad times (recessions) are equally likely. If there are no price level changes β and 1 are the only two possible outcomes for the capital productivity. In this case capital productivity and capital return are the same. The parameter α (where $\alpha > 1$) captures the effect of price level changes on the return on capital. The parameter α depends positively on the size of the capital gains tax and the magnitude of the price level changes.[11] With this minimum of two parameters we can model the effects on the return on capital in the six states of an economy. The role of β has already been explained. The parameter α is used in the following way: capital productivity is divided by α in times of inflation and multiplied by α in times of deflation. This lowers the return in the first case and raises it in the latter case. The return on capital in the six states a country can assume is depicted in table 2.2.

We look at values of α close to one (i. e., small price level fluctuations) so that we can approximate the expected return on capital by $0.5(\beta + 1)$. It is clear that the most productive state of the economy is the combination boom/deflation. The worst possible outcome is the combination recession/inflation. This is the only state where less than the forgone consumption of the first period can be consumed in the second period. The internationally active investor is, of course, interested in the return on an internationally

---

[11] Under the monetary regimes investigated here the band of the price level movements depends on the difference in output between boom and recession. Hence, α depends positively on β. It follows that it would make no sense to simulate changes in β while holding α constant.

Table 2.2 Return on Capital in the Different States of a Country's Economy

	Boom/Inflation	Boom/Stable Price Level	Boom/Deflation	Recession/Inflation	Recession/Stable Price Level	Recession/Deflation
Return	$\dfrac{\beta}{\alpha}$	β	$\beta\alpha$	$\dfrac{1}{\alpha}$	1	α

diversified portfolio. This return depends on the level of investment in the two countries (I^A and I^B) as well as on the states of the two economies. The total return on investment in all possible states of the world can be represented in the form of a payoff matrix. Table 2.3 shows this payoff matrix.

In order to fully specify the maximization problem we need to allocate probabilities to the 36 states of the world. These probabilities are depicted in table 2.4. It is interesting to note that although we have 36 states of the world we only need to specify 12 different probabilities. Due to the fact that all probabilities must add up to one we could even reduce this number to 11. The reason for the reduction in the number of probabilities is quite straightforward. The first point to note is that, since the countries are identical, the matrix must be symmetrical with respect to the main diagonal. This means, for example, that it is equally likely that we have boom/deflation in country A combined with boom/inflation in country B or boom/inflation in country A combined with boom/ deflation in country B.

Second, I also claim that the matrix of probabilities is symmetric with respect to the second diagonal. This means, for example, that the probability of the event that we have boom and inflation in both countries is the same as the probability that we find recession and deflation in both places. It will become clear in the description of the various regimes that this depends on an assumption of policy symmetry. What do we know about the values of the probabilities πA, πB, πC, πD, πE, πF, πG, πH, πI, πK, πL, and πM? What are they related to? This can best be understood by realizing that the primary driving force in this model is changes in business conditions (i. e., variations in productivity). These variations in productivity are connected between countries. Specifically, we assume a constant correlation [$\sigma = Corr(CP^A, CP^B)$] between the capital productivities (CP^A and CP^B) of the two economies. It is assumed that this correlation is not affected by the choice of monetary regime. Empirically, we would expect the correlation to be positive.[12] Cyclical movements in output are at least partly driven by forces that operate internationally (like changes in raw material prices and linkages through foreign trade) and thus have a tendency to co-move between countries.

---

[12] See Kupiec (1991).

Table 2.3 The Investment Payoff Matrix

Country A Country B	Boom/ Inflation	Boom/ Stable Price Level	Boom/ Deflation	Recession/ Inflation	Recession/ Stable Price Level	Recession/ Deflation
Boom/ Inflation	$\frac{\beta}{\alpha}(I^A + I^B)$	$\beta I^A + \frac{\beta}{\alpha}I^B$	$\beta\alpha I^A + \frac{\beta}{\alpha}I^B$	$\frac{1}{\alpha}I^A + \frac{\beta}{\alpha}I^B$	$I^A + \frac{\beta}{\alpha}I^B$	$\alpha I^A + \frac{\beta}{\alpha}I^B$
Boom/ Stable Price Level	$\frac{\beta}{\alpha}I^A + \beta I^B$	$\beta(I^A + I^B)$	$\beta\alpha I^A + \beta I^B$	$\frac{1}{\alpha}I^A + \beta I^B$	$I^A + \beta I^B$	$\alpha I^A + \beta I^B$
Boom/ Deflation	$\frac{\beta}{\alpha}I^A + \beta\alpha I^B$	$\beta I^A + \beta\alpha I^B$	$\beta\alpha(I^A + I^B)$	$\frac{1}{\alpha}I^A + \beta\alpha I^B$	$I^A + \beta\alpha I^B$	$\alpha I^A + \beta\alpha I^B$
Recession Inflation	$\frac{\beta}{\alpha}I^A + \frac{1}{\alpha}I^B$	$\beta I^A + \frac{1}{\alpha}I^B$	$\beta\alpha I^A + \frac{1}{\alpha}I^B$	$\frac{1}{\alpha}(I^A + I^B)$	$I^A + \frac{1}{\alpha}I^B$	$\alpha I^A + \frac{1}{\alpha}I^B$
Recession Stable Price Level	$\frac{\beta}{\alpha}I^A + I^B$	$\beta I^A + I^B$	$\beta\alpha I^A + I^B$	$\frac{1}{\alpha}I^A + I^B$	$I^A + I^B$	$\alpha I^A + I^B$
Recession Deflation	$\frac{\beta}{\alpha}I^A + \alpha I^B$	$\beta I^A + \alpha I^B$	$\beta\alpha I^A + \alpha I^B$	$\frac{1}{\alpha}I^A + \alpha I^B$	$I^A + \alpha I^B$	$\alpha(I^A + I^B)$

Table 2.4 The Matrix of Probabilities

Country A	Boom/ Inflation	Boom/ Stable Price Level	Boom/ Deflation	Recession/ Inflation	Recession/ Stable Price Level	Recession/ Deflation
Country B						
Boom/ Inflation	πA	πB	πC	πD	πE	πF
Boom/ Stable Price Level	πB	πG	πH	πI	πK	πE
Boom/ Deflation	πC	πH	πL	πM	πI	πD
Recession/ Inflation	πD	πI	πM	πL	πH	πC
Recession Stable Price Level	πE	πK	πI	πH	πG	πB
Recession/ Deflation	πF	πE	πD	πC	πB	πA

From the correlation mentioned above one can immediately derive probabilities for a state matrix. Table 2.5 shows this probability matrix. It is clear that the two matrices in tables 2.4 and 2.5. are connected. The probability denoted by τ in table 2.5 is the sum of the nine probabilities in the upper left-hand corner and also equal to the sum of the nine probabilities in the lower right-hand corner of table 2.4. Moreover, the sum of the nine probabilities in the upper right-hand corner and the sum of the probabilities in the lower left-hand corner in table 2.4 have to add up to $0.5 - \tau$. This follows because of the symmetry condition and because all probabilities add up to one. We connect the probabilities of the state matrix with the exogenously given correlation between capital productivities by noting that the probability of having a boom (or a recession) in both countries at the same time (τ) stands in an arithmetically simple relationship to the correlation coefficient.[13] The table states this relationship. While the correlation σ ranges between -1 and 1 the probability τ ranges between 0 and 0.5. If, for example, the correlation between capital productivities were zero the four states of the table would have equal probabilities of 0.25 each. On the other hand, a correlation coefficient of one would imply that with probability 0.5 there is a boom and with probability 0.5 there is a recession in both countries. In the following we will mostly use the probability τ instead of the correlation coefficient. The exogenously given correlation between capital productivities thus fully determines the probabilities of the four states of table 2.5. In order to make a further differentiation into probabilities of the finer grid of states of table 2.4 it is necessary to consider each of the monetary regimes in turn.

---

[13] The covariance between country A's and country B's capital productivity is
$$Cov(CP^A, CP^B) = E\{[CP^A - E(CP^A)][CP^B - E(CP^B)]\}$$
$$= \tau[\beta - 0.5(\beta + 1)][\beta - 0.5(\beta + 1)] + \tau[1 - 0.5(\beta + 1)][1 - 0.5(\beta + 1)]$$
$$+ (0.5 - \tau)[\beta - 0.5(\beta + 1)][1 - 0.5(\beta + 1)] + (0.5 - \tau)[1 - 0.5(\beta + 1)][\beta - 0.5(\beta + 1)]$$
$$= 2(2\tau - 0.5)[0.5(1 - \beta)]^2.$$

Since the standard deviations of the two productivities are the same $Std(CP^A) = Std(CP^B) = 0.5(\beta - 1)$ the correlation coefficient between the two is just $Corr(CP^A, CP^B) = \sigma = Cov(CP^A, CP^B)/[Std(CP^A) \cdot Std(CP^B)] = 4\tau - 1$. Thus, the expression stated in table 2.5 (i. e., $\tau = 0.25 + 0.25\sigma$) follows.

Table 2.5 Probability Matrix for Business Conditions

Country A	Boom	Recession
Country B		
Boom	$\tau = 0.25 + 0.25\sigma$	$0.5 - \tau = 0.25 - 0.25\sigma$
Recession	$0.5 - \tau = 0.25 - 0.25\sigma$	$\tau = 0.25 + 0.25\sigma$

2.2 Monetary Regimes

In this section I will discuss four commonly known monetary regimes. Given the simple account of the working of the two economies and the investor's situation the monetary regimes are also highly stylized. Many practical issues of importance for administrating these regimes are not dealt with. Instead, the regimes are reduced to their bare essentials. The four regimes are the regime of money stock fixing, the one-sided exchange rate peg, the two-sided exchange rate peg, and the regime of price level fixing. At the end of section 2.3, which compares these monetary regimes, I will outline a fifth regime designed to perform best under the circumstances described. It is assumed that investors know the monetary regime under which they have to operate. Hence, there is no regime uncertainty. This means that problems of policy commitment and dynamic consistency are not investigated here.

A technical point at the beginning: the earlier description of the states of the world indicated that price level increases and decreases are equal in absolute terms. Hence, we describe a situation with zero expected inflation. This implies that the central banks manipulate their money stock under any regime such that the expected price level in period two equals the price level of period one. This is particularly important when we think of the policy of money stock fixing. In our setup this cannot mean that the money stock remains unchanged from period one to period two. Instead, fixing the money stock in this environment means that the money stock for period two is chosen from the outset and is not changed in the light of information on the state of the world in period two. Money stock targeting is in fact the only regime discussed here where the central banks do not use information on the state of the economy for setting the policy in the second period.[14]

---

[14] It is obvious that the second period money stock under any regime tends to be lower than that in the first period since income in the second period is only a fraction of that of the first period. Since the price level in period two depends on production in period two and the latter, in turn, depends on investment, it seems impossible to set the money stock that produces zero expected inflation before the private sector has made its investment decision. However, this is not so. The individual does not take into account his investment decision's impact on the price level, which he takes as exogenous. Thus, a central bank can calculate the individual's maximization problem under any monetary regime and also calculate the level of investment the individual will choose. With that knowledge, the central bank can set the money stock so as to be consistent with the aim of zero expected inflation.

We now consider in detail this regime of money stock fixing or targeting. It is called the $\overline{M}$-regime. As mentioned before a central bank is understood to operate the $\overline{M}$-regime when it keeps the money stock unchanged from period one to period two except for the change necessary to avoid a predictable price level change. When period two brings about a boom (recession) then the price level necessarily drops (rises) under this regime. This implies that the price level always moves countercyclically which means that only states with boom/deflation and recession/inflation are possible. All other states have a zero probability. In this case the probability matrix is the one shown in table 2.6. It is clear that this matrix is essentially the same as the one shown in table 2.5. The price level movement is directly attached to the state of business conditions. The entries with zeros are states that are never realized under the $\overline{M}$-regime. It is easy to see that under the monetary regime described there is a chance of the exchange rate remaining constant. This probability is 2τ. An unchanging exchange rate results in the two states where both countries either experience inflation or deflation. The exchange rate does not remain fixed when one country experiences a boom while the other is in recession. Hence, the exchange rate changes from period one to period two with probability $1-2\tau$.

Under a fixed exchange rate regime there are states of the world where at least one country must change its money stock. The regime called the $\overline{E}1$-regime is a one-sided peg where one country follows the $\overline{M}$-regime and the second country adjusts its monetary policy in order to prevent a change in the exchange rate. Under this regime the price levels of the two countries co-move perfectly and have the same variance as under the $\overline{M}$-regime. It is assumed that only one country makes the adjustment but that either country is equally likely to do so. This is like an agreement that when an activist policy is needed a fair coin is flipped to determine which central bank has to change its money stock.[15] For the probability matrix this implies that with half the probability of the combination recession/inflation with boom/deflation we now have either the combination recession/inflation with boom/inflation or the combination recession/ deflation with boom/deflation. In the first case the country experiencing a boom increases its money stock. In the second case the country experiencing a recession lowers its money stock. This means that states

---

[15] It would not make any material difference if it were clear from the outset which country makes the adjustment. This, however, would mean a deviation from the procedure of treating both countries as identical and having symmetrical probability matrices.

Table 2.6 The Matrix of Probabilities for the $\overline{M}$-regime

Country A	Boom/ Inflation	Boom/ Stable Price Level	Boom/ Deflation	Recession/ Inflation	Recession/ Stable Price Level	Recession/ Deflation
Country B						
Boom/ Inflation	0	0	0	0	0	0
Boom/ Stable Price Level	0	0	0	0	0	0
Boom/ Deflation	0	0	τ	$0.5 - \tau$	0	0
Recession/ Inflation	0	0	$0.5 - \tau$	τ	0	0
Recession Stable Price Level	0	0	0	0	0	0
Recession/ Deflation	0	0	0	0	0	0

involving inflation in one country and deflation in the other occur with zero probability. The resulting probabilities are shown in table 2.7. Instead of the instances of diverging price level movements we now have equally often (i. e., determined by the flip of the coin) either inflation or deflation in both countries. The case of the $\bar{E}1$-regime exemplifies the symmetry of the matrix of probabilities with respect to the second diagonal. A comparison with table 2.6 makes clear that the difference of the $\bar{E}1$-regime to the $\bar{M}$-regime consists of splitting in half the two instances of the state probability πM and assigning the halves to the four instances of πD.

The second regime with a fixed exchange rate - the two-sided peg - is called the $\bar{E}2$-regime. Under this regime, both countries follow a strategy of fixing the money supply but there is policy coordination in states in which inflation rates would differ between the two countries. In these cases both countries adjust their money supply by an equal amount in order to keep the exchange rate fixed. This implies that in these states - one country experiencing a boom and the other experiencing a recession - both countries change their money stock in such a way as to stabilize their price levels. It follows that, compared to the $\bar{M}$-regime and the $\bar{E}1$-regime, the $\bar{E}2$-regime has a lower variance of the price level. The $\bar{E}2$-regime consists of a partial stabilization of price level movements in both countries. Due to the money stock adjustments in the states indicated above, the price level varies only in states where both countries either go through a boom or a recession. In these cases the price level moves by exactly the same amount as under the $\bar{M}$-regime. The probability matrix applicable to this regime is shown in table 2.8. A comparison with table 2.6 shows the difference between the $\bar{E}2$-regime and the $\bar{M}$-regime. Under the latter regime state K (occurring with probability πK) is entered with the probability with which state M (occurring with probability πM) is entered in the former regime.

The fourth monetary regime considered is the regime of price level fixing. We call this the $\bar{P}$-regime. Here, the central banks raise their money stock in the second period if a boom occurs and lower it if there is a recession. As a result, entries in the probability matrix denoting states with price level variations all have zero probability. The possible states are indicated in table 2.9. The only non-zero probabilities are πG and πK. They are quantitatively the same as the probabilities of the combinations boom/boom, boom/recession, recession/boom, recession/recession in table 2.5. Because we have a one-good model it turns out that the $\bar{P}$-regime also leads to a constant exchange rate. Thus, in one sense the $\bar{P}$-regime can be seen as a variation of the $\bar{E}2$-regime

Table 2.7 The Matrix of Probabilities for the $\bar{E}1$-Regime

Country B \ Country A	Boom/Inflation	Boom/Stable Price Level	Boom/Deflation	Recession/Inflation	Recession/Stable Price Level	Recession/Deflation
Boom/Inflation	0	0	0	$0.5(0.5-\tau)$	0	0
Boom/Stable Price Level	0	0	0	0	0	0
Boom/Deflation	0	0	τ	0	0	$0.5(0.5-\tau)$
Recession/Inflation	$0.5(0.5-\tau)$	0	0	τ	0	0
Recession/Stable Price Level	0	0	0	0	0	0
Recession/Deflation	0	0	$0.5(0.5-\tau)$	0	0	0

Table 2.8 The Matrix of Probabilities for the $\bar{E}2$-Regime

Country A	Boom/ Inflation	Boom/ Stable Price Level	Boom/ Deflation	Recession/ Inflation	Recession/ Stable Price Level	Recession/ Deflation
Country B						
Boom/ Inflation	0	0	0	0	0	0
Boom/ Stable Price Level	0	0	0	0	$0.5 - \tau$	0
Boom/ Deflation	0	0	τ	0	0	0
Recession/ Inflation	0	0	0	τ	0	0
Recession Stable Price Level	0	$0.5 - \tau$	0	0	0	0
Recession/ Deflation	0	0	0	0	0	0

Table 2.9 The Matrix of Probabilities for the $\bar{P}$-Regime

Country A Country B	Boom/ Inflation	Boom/ Stable Price Level	Boom/ Deflation	Recession/ Inflation	Recession/ Stable Price Level	Recession/ Deflation
Boom/ Inflation	0	0	0	0	0	0
Boom/ Stable Price Level	0	τ	0	0	$0.5 - \tau$	0
Boom/ Deflation	0	0	0	0	0	0
Recession/ Inflation	0	0	0	0	0	0
Recession Stable Price Level	0	$0.5 - \tau$	0	0	τ	0
Recession/ Deflation	0	0	0	0	0	0

(i. e., the regime that reduces the price level variance to zero). There is, however, a minor logical difference between the regimes in that under the $\overline{P}$-regime none of the central banks has to care or know about what is going on abroad.

2.3 Solutions

The problem of finding explicit solutions for the values of I^A and I^B for the four monetary regimes can be solved for the case of a quadratic utility function $u(c) = ac - bc^2$ (applicable to levels of $c < a/2b$). For this purpose the payoff values under each regime multiplied by the probabilities of their occurrence are used to derive the expected utility in (2.1). The resulting first order conditions for I^A and I^B are linear. Appendix 2.A shows - for the examples of the $\overline{M}$-regime and the $\overline{E}1$-regime - the optimality conditions for the $\overline{M}$-regime and the solutions for the optimal I^A and I^B. As is well known the quadratic utility function has the implausible feature that both the relative and the absolute risk aversion increase with the increase in wealth.[16] As will become clear the present case is one where this feature of the quadratic utility function leads to a different conclusion regarding investment compared to that which results from a utility function with constant relative risk aversion.[17]

When individuals have a utility function different from the quadratic case the impact of the various monetary regimes on investment and welfare has to be assessed in an indirect way. Explicit solutions for I^A and I^B cannot be reached. To proceed in this case we build on the fact that the investment opportunities in the two countries are equally attractive to all investors. Hence, any optimal portfolio will contain equal amounts of domestic and foreign investments.[18] This means that savings are allocated equally to both domestic and foreign investment. The return on one unit of this optimally diversified portfolio is henceforth denoted by R_s. Moreover, we have assumed that the monetary regimes do not affect the expected return on either investment project. What counts then for investment and welfare is the variance of R_s

---

[16] See Blanchard and Fischer (1989, p. 288).

[17] It is well known that the effect of return uncertainty on savings is ambiguous. See Drèze and Modigliani (1972) and Hey (1979).

[18] This can also be seen in the solutions for the quadratic case in appendix 2.A where the solutions for I^A and I^B are identical.

under different monetary regimes. The ordering of these variances is depicted in table 2.10. Appendix 2.B contains the calculated values of the variances and proofs of their relative sizes. The variances are calculated for an investment unit consisting of half a domestic and half a foreign investment unit.

Table 2.10 Portfolio Variance under Different Monetary Regimes*

$$Var(R_s)_{\bar{E}1} \geq Var(R_s)_{\bar{M}} \geq Var(R_s)_{\bar{E}2} > Var(R_s)_{\bar{P}}$$

* $\bar{E}1$, $\bar{M}$, $\bar{E}2$, and $\bar{P}$ indicate the regimes of the one-sided exchange rate peg, of money stock control, of the two-sided peg, and of price level control, respectively.

The $\bar{E}1$-regime leads to the highest portfolio variance, followed by the $\bar{M}$-regime, the $\bar{E}2$-regime, and the $\bar{P}$-regime with the lowest variance. The differences between $Var(R_s)_{\bar{E}1}$, $Var(R_s)_{\bar{M}}$, and $Var(R_s)_{\bar{E}2}$ reduce to zero when productivities become perfectly positively correlated between countries. Clearly, with perfectly synchronous business conditions (i. e., $\sigma = 1$ or, equivalently, $\tau = 0.5$) the $\bar{M}$-regime produces a fixed exchange rate (i. e., the same outcome as the $\bar{E}1$- and the $\bar{E}2$-regimes). The $\bar{P}$-regime, however, distances itself further from the other regimes in terms of the portfolio variance the closer σ is to one (for details see appendix 2.B).

The welfare ordering is straightforward: as is common, this ordering follows the level of expected utility [see Helpman and Razin (1982)]. With equal expected returns the superior regime is the one with the lower portfolio variance. Thus, the regime of fixing the price level is the best choice in the present case. As with the variances before, the welfare differences between regimes also depend on the correlation between the capital productivities of the countries. The welfare ordering of the regimes is highlighted in table 2.11.

Table 2.11 Welfare under Different Monetary Regimes*

$$E(U)_{\overline{P}} > E(U)_{\overline{E2}} \geq E(U)_{\overline{M}} \geq E(U)_{\overline{E1}}$$

* $\overline{P}$, $\overline{E2}$, $\overline{M}$, and $\overline{E1}$ indicate the regimes of price level control, the two-sided exchange rate peg, money stock control, and the one-sided peg, respectively.

In order to asses the effect of the various monetary regimes on investment via the portfolio variance we make use of a device used by Sandmo (1970) in a similar context. The utility function assumed from now on is of the constant relative risk aversion type, that is, $u(c) = (c^{1-\theta} - 1)/(1 - \theta)$ with $\theta > 0$ (where θ is the coefficient of relative risk aversion and $\theta = 0$ indicates risk neutrality) and $u(c) = \log(c)$ for $\theta = 1$. As discussed before, savings are allocated equally between domestic and foreign investment. Hence, it suffices to know how savings react to an increase in the portfolio variance. Following Sandmo we replace R_s by $\overline{R} + \gamma(R_s - \overline{R})$ where $\overline{R}$ is the expected value of R_s. An increase in γ now indicates an increase in portfolio variance. Hence, the first order condition for c_1 (the consumption in the first of the two periods) $u'(c_1) = \rho E \{R_s u'[R_s(1 - c_1)]\}$ can be rewritten as

$$u'(c_1) = \rho E \{[\overline{R} + \gamma(R_s - \overline{R})]u'[[\overline{R} + \gamma(R_s - \overline{R})](1 - c_1)]\}.$$

Differentiating both sides with respect to γ and using the expression for the coefficient of relative risk aversion $\theta = -u''c/u'$ we find:

$$\frac{\partial c_1}{\partial \gamma} = -\frac{\partial s}{\partial \gamma} = \frac{(1-\theta)\rho E[(R_s - \overline{R})u'_2]}{u''_1 + \rho E u''_2 R_s^2}. \qquad (2.2)$$

For the case $\theta = 1$ (i. e., the log utility function) we have certainty equivalence: an increase in portfolio variance does not affect the first period's consumption.

Hence, it does not affect savings and investment. In this case the choice of monetary regime is of no consequence for the level of investment. This neutrality does, of course, not apply to welfare which still decreases with a rising portfolio variance.

For the more plausible case of $\theta > 1$, the effect of a higher portfolio variance is to decrease consumption (increase savings).[19] This follows because $E[(R_s - \bar{R})u'_2]$ is negative. Hence, investment is highest under the $\bar{E}1$-regime and lowest under the $\bar{P}$-regime. The complete ordering is shown in table 2.12. Using the quadratic utility function and going through the same steps that lead to (2.2) results in the exact reverse ordering of regimes to that depicted in table 2.12. Given the above mentioned implausible feature of the quadratic utility function, I suggest the ordering of table 2.12.

Table 2.12 Investment under Different Monetary Regimes: the Case where the Coefficient of Relative Risk Aversion is above One*

$$I_{\bar{E}1} \geq I_{\bar{M}} \geq I_{\bar{E}2} > I_{\bar{P}}$$

* $\bar{E}1$, $\bar{M}$, $\bar{E}2$, and $\bar{P}$ indicate the regimes of the one-sided exchange rate peg, of money stock control, of the two-sided peg, and of price level control, respectively.

---

[19] Empirical estimates of θ (the coefficient of relative risk aversion) are usually well above one. Hall (1988) estimates θ looking at the relationship between consumption growth and the expected real interest rate. All his estimates lie above one with a third of them close to three. He rightly points out that his procedure in effect leads to an estimate of the intertemporal elasticity of substitution and that the coefficient of relative risk aversion is the reciprocal of the intertemporal elasticity of substitution only in the case of an additive utility function. However, Seldon (1979), in a more general formulation of preferences, shows that it is indeed the intertemporal elasticity of substitution which is decisive for the effect of return risk on savings. Frankel (1986), upon review of the literature, uses a value of $\theta = 2$ for his simulations.

According to Aizenman's (1992) analysis, investment under a fixed exchange rate is always higher than under a flexible exchange rate. The present result contrasts with this view: the only regime implying a fixed exchange rate that leads to higher investment than under a regime of money stock fixing (with a flexible exchange rate) is the regime of the one-sided exchange rate peg. However, if the exchange rate is fixed by a two-sided peg or if it is constant because the two countries fix their price levels, investment is lower than under a flexible exchange rate. None of the results presented would be qualitatively altered in the presence of a positive second period endowment. In case the second period endowment is stochastic - for example, each individual gets a fixed endowment in domestic nominal terms - the individuals would pool their risk by exchanging half their endowment for half the endowment of the foreigners. This is the case studied by Lucas (1982).

The results, however, would be altered if we had the unlikely case of a positive instead of a negative correlation between the after-tax return on investment and inflation. This could occur as mentioned earlier if the corporate tax structure permits an interest deduction that also includes the inflation component. If this effect were to outweigh the effect of the tax on nominal capital gains there would indeed be $\alpha < 1$. In this case the ordering of monetary regimes with respect to portfolio variance would change. While the result $Var(R_s)_{\overline{E1}} \geq Var(R_s)_{\overline{M}} \geq Var(R_s)_{\overline{E2}}$ would still hold, the inequality $Var(R_s)_{\overline{E2}} > Var(R_s)_{\overline{P}}$ would be reversed. Under these circumstances the correlation between the productivities would determine where $Var(R_s)_{\overline{P}}$ would range relative to the variances under the three other regimes. With perfectly negative correlation (i. e., $\tau = 0$) the ordering would be the same as in table 2.10. With perfectly positive correlation (i. e., $\tau = 0.5$) the $Var(R_s)_{\overline{P}}$ would be the highest of the four regimes. Hence, with $\alpha < 1$, the rating of regimes for welfare and the level of investment would depend on the correlation between the productivities of the two countries.

Besides the regimes discussed so far we can also think about the design of an optimal monetary regime. Clearly, the optimal monetary regime would be the one that produces zero variance of the return on investment. In the case where $\alpha > 1$ this would imply a monetary policy that would result in inflation in boom states and deflation in recession states. This optimal regime would clearly imply a flexible exchange rate. The procyclical price level movement would be calibrated such that its effect on the return on investment (α^*) would exactly neutralize the variations in productivity (i. e., $\alpha^* = \sqrt{\beta}$).[20] Again, the unlikely case of $\alpha < 1$ points in a different direction. In this case the optimal monetary policy would result in deflation in boom states and inflation in recession states. The price level movement would be calibrated in a fashion similar to that described above (i. e., $\alpha^* = 1/\sqrt{\beta}$).

2.4 Conclusions

This chapter presents an analysis of the effects of the choice of monetary regime on investment and welfare in a two-country model. The study focuses on the effect of the regime choice that works via the variance of the return on investment. Hence, issues involving price rigidities, unemployment, deviations from purchasing power parity, and many others that bear on the choice of monetary regime are ignored here. With this caveat in mind, several conclusions for monetary policy can be drawn from this analysis. These conclusions rest on the non-neutrality of the after-tax return on investment with respect to inflation. Independent of the direction of the tax effect, moving from a regime of money stock control to fixing the exchange rate makes sense only when the variance of the return on the internationally diversified portfolio is reduced in the process. This happens only when international policy coordination is adopted, that is, when a two-sided instead of just a one-sided exchange rate peg is chosen.

In the likely case where the after-tax return on investment depends negatively on the inflation rate the regime of price level control leads to a smaller portfolio variance than the regimes of money stock fixing or exchange rate fixing. In our model, higher return uncertainty drives up precautionary savings and, hence, investment. Among the standard regimes considered, price level fixing is thus the regime that leads to the highest level of welfare and to the lowest level of investment. The more closely business conditions are correlated between countries the more price level fixing stands out as the best monetary regime.

---

[20] Non-stochastic returns on investment also imply that there is no need for international portfolio diversification.

Appendix 2.A: Closed Form Solutions for the Quadratic Case

In this appendix we derive explicit solutions for investment using the quadratic utility function. The resulting first order conditions for I^A and I^B are linear. As an example, the first order condition for the $\overline{M}$-regime is shown in table 2.A1. It is clear from the symmetry of the matrix consisting of the second derivatives, the cross derivatives and the fact that the vectors on the right-hand side of the equations consist of two identical terms that the solution must be $I^A = I^B$. This means that savings are allocated in equal proportions to domestic and to foreign investment. The resulting equations for investment under the various regimes are rather complicated. As an example, table 2.A2 shows the resulting expressions for I^A and I^B for the $\overline{M}$-regime and the $\overline{E}1$-regime. Therefore, despite the explicit solutions available, a numerical simulation is needed to confirm what is more easily established using Sandmo's procedure.

Table 2.A1 First Order Conditions for the $\overline{M}$-regime*

$$\begin{bmatrix} \dfrac{2b}{\alpha^2} \begin{bmatrix} \alpha^2 + \dfrac{\rho}{2}(\alpha^4\beta^2 + 1) & 2\alpha^2\rho\beta(\tfrac{1}{2}-\tau) + \rho\tau(\alpha^4\beta^2+1) + \alpha^2 \\ 2\alpha^2\rho\beta(\tfrac{1}{2}-\tau) + \rho\tau(\alpha^4\beta^2+1) + \alpha^2 & \alpha^2 + \dfrac{\rho}{2}(\alpha^4\beta^2+1) \end{bmatrix} \end{bmatrix} \begin{bmatrix} I^A \\ I^B \end{bmatrix} = \begin{bmatrix} 2b + \dfrac{a\rho(\alpha^2\beta+1)}{2\alpha} - a \\ 2b + \dfrac{a\rho(\alpha^2\beta+1)}{2\alpha} - a \end{bmatrix}$$

* $\overline{M}$ indicates the regime of money stock targeting.

Table 2.A2 Investment (Domestic and Foreign) under Two Monetary Regimes*

$$I^A_{\overline{M}} = I^B_{\overline{M}} = \dfrac{\alpha\left[\alpha(4b-2a) + a\rho(\alpha^2\beta+1)\right]}{2b\left[2\rho\tau(\alpha^4\beta^2 - 2\alpha^2\beta+1) + \alpha^2(\alpha^2\rho\beta^2 + 2\rho\beta + 4) + \rho\right]}$$

$$I^A_{\overline{E1}} = I^B_{\overline{E1}} = \dfrac{\alpha\left\{a\rho\left[\tfrac{\tau}{2}(1-\alpha^2+\alpha^2\beta-\beta) + \tfrac{1}{4}(\alpha^2+1)(\beta+1)\right] - a\alpha + 2b\alpha\right\}}{b\left\{\rho\tau(3-\alpha^4+3\alpha^4\beta^2-\beta^2-2\alpha^4\beta-2\beta) + \tfrac{1}{2}\alpha^2[\alpha^2(\rho+2\rho\beta)+8] + \tfrac{1}{2}\rho(\alpha^4\beta^2+\beta^2+2\beta+1)\right\}}$$

* $\overline{M}$ and $\overline{E}1$ indicate the regime of money stock targeting and the regime of the one-sided peg.

Appendix 2.B: Portfolio Variance under Different Monetary Regimes

In this appendix the values for the portfolio variance under alternative monetary regimes are given.

$$Var(R_s)_{\overline{E1}} = \tau\{[\beta\alpha - 0.5(\beta + 1)]^2 + [\frac{1}{\alpha} - 0.5(\beta + 1)]^2\}$$
$$+ (0.5 - \tau)[0.5(\frac{1}{\alpha} + \frac{\beta}{\alpha}) - 0.5(\beta + 1)]^2$$
$$+ (0.5 - \tau)[0.5(\alpha + \beta\alpha) - 0.5(\beta + 1)]^2$$

$$Var(R_s)_{\overline{M}} = \tau\{[\beta\alpha - 0.5(\beta + 1)]^2 + [\frac{1}{\alpha} - 0.5(\beta + 1)]^2\}$$
$$+ 2(0.5 - \tau)[0.5(\frac{1}{\alpha} + \beta\alpha) - 0.5(\beta + 1)]^2$$

$$Var(R_s)_{\overline{E2}} = \tau\{[\beta\alpha - 0.5(\beta + 1)]^2 + [\frac{1}{\alpha} - 0.5(\beta + 1)]^2\}$$

$$Var(R_s)_{\overline{P}} = \tau\{[\beta - 0.5(\beta + 1)]^2 + [1 - 0.5(\beta + 1)]^2\} = 0.5\,\tau\,(\beta - 1)^2$$

The variances for the $\overline{E2}$- and the $\overline{P}$-regime have fewer terms because under these regimes there are two states where R_s is equal to its expected value. The size ordering can be accomplished by looking at the differences of the variances:

$$Var(R_s)_{\overline{E1}} - Var(R_s)_{\overline{M}} = 0.25(0.5 - \tau)\left[\left(\frac{1}{\alpha} + \frac{\beta}{\alpha} - \beta - 1\right)^2 - \left(\frac{1}{\alpha} + \beta\alpha - \beta - 1\right)^2\right]$$
$$+ 0.25(0.5 - \tau)\left[(\alpha + \beta\alpha - \beta - 1)^2 - \left(\frac{1}{\alpha} + \beta\alpha - \beta - 1\right)^2\right]$$
$$= 0.25(0.5 - \tau)\left[\left(\frac{1}{\alpha} - 1\right)^2(1 + \beta)^2 - \left(\beta - \frac{1}{\alpha}\right)^2(\alpha - 1)^2\right]$$
$$+ 0.25(0.5 - \tau)\left[(\alpha - 1)^2(1 + \beta)^2 - \left(\beta - \frac{1}{\alpha}\right)^2(\alpha - 1)^2\right]$$

Since for values of α around 1 we have approximately $\left(\frac{1}{\alpha} - 1\right)^2 = (\alpha - 1)^2$ we can write the above expression as

$$Var(R_s)_{\overline{E}1} - Var(R_s)_{\overline{M}} = 0.5\,(0.5 - \tau)\,(\alpha - 1)^2\,[(1 + \beta)^2 - (\beta - \tfrac{1}{\alpha})^2] \geq 0 \ .$$

This difference is definitely non-negative because

$$0.5 - \tau \geq 0,\ (\alpha - 1)^2 > 0,\ (1 + \beta)^2 > 4 \text{ and } (\beta - \tfrac{1}{\alpha})^2 < 1 \ .$$

In turn, we have

$$Var(R_s)_{\overline{M}} - Var(R_s)_{\overline{E}2} = 0.5\,(0.5 - \tau)\,[(\tfrac{1}{\alpha} + \beta\alpha) - (\beta + 1)]^2 \geq 0 \ .$$

This is definitely non-negative because the term in the second set of brackets is squared. It is apparent from the expressions stated above that the three variances involved are equal when business conditions between countries are perfectly positively correlated (i. e., when $\tau = 0.5$). Hence, the choice of one of the three regimes has a greater effect when capital productivities are weakly (or negatively) correlated.

Last, the difference $Var(R_s)_{\overline{E}2} - Var(R_s)_{\overline{P}}$ is positive because the terms in brackets in the expression for $Var(R_s)_{\overline{E}2}$ are larger than in $Var(R_s)_{\overline{P}}$ because

$$\beta\alpha > \beta > 0.5(\beta + 1) > 1 > \frac{1}{\alpha} \ .$$

With similar reasoning it can be shown that all variances increase with an increase in τ. Contrary to the previous comparisons of variances, $Var(R_s)_{\overline{E}2} - Var(R_s)_{\overline{P}}$ rises as τ rises. This means that, as the differences between the $\overline{E}1$-, $\overline{E}2$-, and the $\overline{M}$-regime become negligible (i. e., as τ goes to 0.5), the advantage of the $\overline{P}$-regime over the other regimes becomes ever more pronounced.

3

Exchange Rate Risk and International Capital Allocation

This analysis differs from that in chapter 2 in that the focus is on deviations of the exchange rate from purchasing power parity. Variability of the real exchange rate - hence exchange rate risk - is the main theme of this chapter. The topic of the previous chapter, that is inflation uncertainty and the non-neutrality of returns with respect to inflation, thus moves to the background. As suggested in the introductory chapter the models of chapter 2 and 3 are complementary: chapter 2 focuses on the role of inflation risk while chapter 3 focuses on the role of exchange rate risk. The simplest interpretation of the situation presented here is to think of the price levels in the two countries as fixed. Changes in the nominal exchange rate thus automatically translate into variations in the real exchange rate. I do not attempt to model the exchange rate. Rather, the analysis begins with the assertion that the exchange rate regime influences the variability of the exchange rate. The model assumes that the regime of fixing the nominal exchange rate implies zero variations in the real exchange rate. The conclusions of the analysis, however, hold equally if the regime of fixing the nominal exchange rate merely lowers, rather than eliminates, fluctuations in the real exchange rate. This is what the empirical evidence gathered by Mussa (1986) and Eichengreen (1988) suggests.[1]

The model developed in the next section shows how exchange rate uncertainty affects the individual decision to hold domestic or foreign assets and how these decisions in the aggregate determine the allocation of wealth and the yield differentials between countries. Risk aversion plays the key role in this

---

[1] Eichengreen studies real and nominal exchange rates of the inter-war period and concludes that a system of managed floating takes an intermediate position with respect to exchange rate variability.

model. Our analysis thus differs from Aizenman's (1992) recent model where risk-neutral multinational firms make the investment decisions. The present work contrasts with the literature it formally resembles in that it includes physical capital besides bonds.[2] The analysis is conducted using a two-country model.

While the central topic of this chapter is the role of the exchange rate regime in the international allocation of physical capital it also addresses several related issues. First, the model delivers a theory of the foreign exchange risk premium. It provides, along the lines of Frankel (1979) and Grinols and Turnovsky (1991), a condition under which exchange rate risk is fully diversifiable. Second, the model suggests a possible solution to the Feldstein-Horioka (1980) puzzle. Under a flexible exchange rate - so the results confirm - a larger fraction of a country's savings is channeled into domestic investments. Exchange rate risk thus helps to explain the home bias of investment still observed in recent years. Third, it is shown that the choice of exchange rate regime can affect the net foreign asset position of a country. It can happen, for example, that a country that was a net creditor under the fixed exchange rate becomes a net debtor under a regime of floating currencies.

The last part of this chapter discusses how economic efficiency and the distribution of income are affected by the exchange rate regime. These effects play an important role in the political selection of an exchange rate regime. This type of analysis follows MacDougall (1960) and Niehans (1984). It will be assumed that workers and land owners have no financial wealth (i. e., they do not invest) and that investors get all income from their earnings on invested capital. It is shown that labor and land owners on one side and capital on the other side may take opposing views with respect to the exchange rate regime preferred. This type of conflict is already well known from the debate on the liberalization of international capital flows.

3.1 The Individual's Choice

The individual invests his or her wealth at the beginning of the period and consumes the gross return at the end of the period. We assume that risk averse investors can invest in four types of assets. The individual can allocate his wealth between domestic and foreign bonds and domestic and foreign stocks.

---

[2] See, e. g., Dornbusch (1983).

The home country investor earns with certainty a return i in domestic currency on the domestic bond and i^* in foreign currency on the foreign bond. On the domestic equity he earns an uncertain return r (with an expected value of $\bar{r}$ and a variance σ_r^2) in domestic currency and r^* (with $\bar{r}^*$ and $\sigma_{r^*}^2$) in foreign currency on the foreign stock. The returns r and r^* are interchangeably called equity yields, capital returns, and marginal products of capital. The return in domestic currency of the foreign assets is affected by the exchange rate change d which has a mean value of zero (where d denotes an appreciation of the foreign currency). Hence, the returns on the foreign assets measured in domestic currency are $i^* + d$ and $r^* + d$, respectively. The variance of d is σ_d^2. The foreign investor's yield prospects are symmetrical to those of the domestic investor. Measured in her country's currency she earns $r - d$ on an equity in the home country, r^* on the equity of her country, $i - d$ on the home country bond, and i^* on her country's bond. Table 3.1 summarizes the returns the two countries' investors receive in their respective currency.

Table 3.1 Yields from Different Assets in Investor's Currency

		Investors	
		Home	Foreign
	Home Equity	r	$r - d$
	Foreign Equity	$r^* + d$	r^*
Assets	Home Bond	i	$i - d$
	Foreign Bond	$i^* + d$	i^*

In the literature, asset returns are usually deflated with a price index that reflects the investor's consumption preference for the domestic and the foreign good.[3] In the present context we abstract from this consideration and assume that income measured in his or her country's currency enters the investor's von Neuman-Morgenstern utility function.[4] We use a utility function that is quadratic in the end-of-period wealth ($\tilde{w}$). Since the individual maximizes expected utility, the utility function can also be written as a function of expected end-of-period wealth ($\overline{w}$) and the end-of-period variance of wealth ($\sigma_{\tilde{w}}^2$):[5]

$$U = U(\overline{w}, \sigma_{\tilde{w}}^2) \qquad (3.1)$$

The home country investor allocates a fraction x of his wealth (w) to his country's stocks, a fraction y to foreign stocks, a fraction z to foreign bonds and a fraction $1 - x - y - z$ to his country's bonds. The bond market can be used to hedge exchange rate risk on investment in foreign stocks. The investor can fully hedge his holdings of foreign stocks against exchange rate risk by emitting foreign bonds (i. e., by borrowing abroad) to the amount of his holdings of foreign stocks.[6] He then invests the borrowed money in his country's bonds and earns the riskless return i.

It is clear that foreign investments would all be hedged if there were no costs involved. Hedging is costly for investors of one of the two countries when the market determines a non-zero difference between the two countries' bond returns. If $i^* - i > 0$ the domestic investor pays a premium to hedge his currency risk. He receives less on the domestic bonds than he has to pay on his foreign bond debt. It is obvious that the existence of the two bond markets makes a forward exchange market redundant. Instead of selling forward the proceeds of the expected return on his foreign stock holdings the investor engages in the transactions outlined above. If a forward exchange market existed the foreign exchange risk premium determined in that market would be

---

[3] See Dornbusch (1983) and Branson and Henderson (1985).

[4] This formulation makes portfolio decisions independent of the preference for the home good relative to the foreign good.

[5] See appendix 3.A for a derivation of this utility function.

[6] This is only approximately true. The statement neglects the term rd.

strictly equal to the difference in bond returns.[7] Given the adopted conventions the end-of-period wealth can be written as

$$\tilde{w} = xwr + yw(r^* + d) + (1 - x - y - z)wi + zw(i^* + d) . \qquad (3.2)$$

The expected end-of-period wealth is

$$\overline{w} = w[x(\overline{r} - i) + y(\overline{r^*} - i) + z(i^* - i) + i] . \qquad (3.3)$$

When we make the working assumption that $\sigma_r^2 = \sigma_{r^*}^2$ then the variance of end-of-period wealth can be written as

$$\sigma_{\tilde{w}}^2 = w^2[(x^2 + y^2)\sigma_r^2 + 2xy\sigma_{r^*, r} + (y + z)^2 \sigma_d^2)] \qquad (3.4)$$

In this formula one new term appears: the covariance between the two returns ($\sigma_{r^*, r}$). The term $\sigma_{r^*, r}$ is closely tied to the covariance between domestic and foreign business conditions. It is clearly assumed to be positive. The covariances between the two returns and the appreciation of the foreign currency ($\sigma_{r, d}$ and $\sigma_{r^*, d}$, respectively) are assumed to be zero and are suppressed.[8] Under

---

[7] This rests on the assumption that the expected appreciation of the exchange rate and the two inflation rates are zero. The foreign exchange risk premium is defined here as the percentage mark-up of the domestic currency in the forward market above the *expected* spot price of the domestic currency. That is, on the forward exchange market one unit of domestic currency sells for more than the expected value of the domestic currency and the foreign currency sells for less than the expected value of foreign currency. Hence, the domestic investor who hedges his currency exposure by selling his foreign currency earnings forward is expected to lose compared to the situation where he waits and sells on the spot market.

[8] This assumption is not critical for the following analysis. It can be argued, however, that it is plausible because there are two counteractive effects. From the literature on exchange rate dynamics [see, e. g., Niehans (1984)] it could be concluded that an increase in r^* could induce a reshuffling of portfolios that would lead to an appreciation of the foreign currency. This would result in a negative $\sigma_{r, d}$ and a positive $\sigma_{r^*, d}$. This argument is weakened in the present context because a higher return in one period does not imply a higher expected return in the next period. A second effect would tend to make $\sigma_{r, d}$ positive and $\sigma_{r^*, d}$ negative. If profitability of investment rises with a depreciation of the currency then r rises with a positive d while r^* falls (this second effect was pointed out to me by Ronald McKinnon).

strictly fixed exchange rates σ_d^2 is zero since d is always zero. When the investor has a fully hedged foreign investment position (i. e., $y = -z$) then the variance of the exchange rate does not affect the variance of his end-of-period wealth.[9] This means that a fully hedged foreign equity position implies an equally large foreign bond debt. Maximization of the utility function with respect to (3.3) and (3.4) results in a system of equations determining the optimal portfolio shares x, y, and z:

$$\begin{bmatrix} \sigma_r^2 & \sigma_{r*,r} & 0 \\ \sigma_{r*,r} & \sigma_r^2 + \sigma_d^2 & \sigma_d^2 \\ 0 & \sigma_d^2 & \sigma_d^2 \end{bmatrix} \begin{bmatrix} x \\ y \\ z \end{bmatrix} = \begin{bmatrix} \frac{1}{\theta}(\bar{r} - i) \\ \frac{1}{\theta}(\bar{r}^* - i) \\ \frac{1}{\theta}(i^* - i) \end{bmatrix} \quad (3.5)$$

The parameter θ is the measure of relative risk aversion.[10] Let's assume for the moment that $\sigma_d^2 > 0$. In that case the matrix on the left-hand side of (3.5) can be inverted and the resulting values for x, y, and z are:

$$\begin{bmatrix} x \\ y \\ z \end{bmatrix} = \begin{bmatrix} \phi_1 & \phi_2 & -\phi_2 \\ -\phi_2 & -\phi_1 & \phi_1 \\ \phi_2 & \phi_3 & -\phi_1 \end{bmatrix} \begin{bmatrix} (\bar{r} - i) \\ (i^* - i) \\ (\bar{r}^* - i) \end{bmatrix} \quad (3.6)$$

where $\phi_1 = \dfrac{\sigma_r^2}{\theta(\sigma_r^2 - \sigma_{r*,r})(\sigma_r^2 + \sigma_{r*,r})} > 0$, $\phi_2 = \dfrac{\sigma_{r*,r}}{\theta(\sigma_r^2 - \sigma_{r*,r})(\sigma_r^2 + \sigma_{r*,r})} > 0$,

and $\phi_3 = \phi_1 + \dfrac{1}{\theta \sigma_d^2} > 0$.

As mentioned before, the difference $i^* - i$ is the foreign exchange risk premium. This is the premium the domestic investor has to pay to hedge the exchange rate risk on his foreign equity investment. It is intuitively clear that a higher premium induces the domestic investor to hold more domestic stocks

---

[9] Again this is not exactly true: the result follows from approximating $(1+r)(1+d)$ by $1+d+r$.
[10] $\theta = -\dfrac{2U_2 w}{U_1}$. U_1 and U_2 are the partial derivatives of the utility function [see (3.1)] with respect to the first and the second argument. See also appendix 3.A for clarifications regarding θ.

(the partial derivative is ϕ_2) and fewer foreign stocks (the partial derivative is $-\phi_1$). This is because the return on the foreign equity net of the insurance premium for the exchange rate risk is decreased. In the case of a fixed exchange rate (i. e., with $\sigma_d^2 = 0$), (3.5) reduces to a system of equations in x and y. Hence, z is not determined. This simply means that with pegged currencies domestic and foreign bonds are perfect substitutes and thus only the share of wealth in this generic type of bonds (i. e., $1 - x - y$) is determined. This point is taken up again in section 3.2 where the aggregate asset demand functions are discussed.

The optimal portfolio fractions for the foreign investor are similar to the fractions for the domestic investor. The symmetrical expression of (3.6) is:

$$\begin{bmatrix} x^* \\ y^* \\ z^* \end{bmatrix} = \begin{bmatrix} \phi_1 & \phi_2 & -\phi_2 \\ -\phi_2 & -\phi_1 & \phi_1 \\ \phi_2 & \phi_3 & -\phi_1 \end{bmatrix} \begin{bmatrix} (\bar{r}^* - i^*) \\ (i - i^*) \\ (\bar{r} - i^*) \end{bmatrix} \quad (3.7)$$

In order to get an expression in the same arguments as (3.6) we insert i in all parentheses where i^* appears and after collecting terms we find:

$$\begin{bmatrix} x^* \\ y^* \\ z^* \end{bmatrix} = \begin{bmatrix} -\phi_2 & -\phi_1 & \phi_1 \\ \phi_1 & \phi_2 & -\phi_2 \\ -\phi_1 & -\phi_4 & \phi_2 \end{bmatrix} \begin{bmatrix} (\bar{r} - i) \\ (i^* - i) \\ (\bar{r}^* - i) \end{bmatrix} \quad (3.7')$$

with ϕ_1, ϕ_2 as above and $\phi_4 = \phi_2 + \dfrac{1}{\theta \sigma_d^2}$.

A comparison of (3.6) and (3.7') reveals that the fractions of the respective wealth the domestic and the foreign investors want to hold in equity of the same origin are identical (i. e., $x = y^*$ and $y = x^*$). It is clear that the higher a country's stock return the more both countries' investors want of that equity. It is less obvious that the difference between the bond returns $i^* - i$ affects the foreigner's demand for equities in the same way as the domestic investor's demand. However, there is a simple explanation: a positive $i^* - i$ permits the foreign investor to engage in a pair of bond transactions that hedges her exchange rate risk on the equity investment across the border while additionally paying a positive return. Hence, the higher the bond yield difference

$i^* - i$ the more she will favor the other country's equity just as her foreign counterpart does.

The above also implies that both countries' investors hold an identical fraction of their wealth in stocks (i. e., $x + y = x^* + y^*$). The wealth fractions allocated to the bonds of the two denominations are, however, different. The fraction of foreign bonds the foreign investor wants to hold (i. e., $1 - x^* - y^* - z^*$) is equal to one plus the fraction the domestic investor wants to hold in the same asset (i. e., $1 + z$). The next section will discuss in more detail the nature of bond supply and demand.

3.2 Macroeconomic Equilibrium

We now turn to the determination of the capital stocks and the equilibrium bond and equity returns in the two countries. It has to be understood that the capital market described determines equilibrium expected returns. Hence, when the terms 'equity yield', 'capital return', or 'marginal product of capital' are used from now on we mean their expected values. In order to determine market equilibrium we have to make the step from individual behavior to aggregate behavior. In this context this first of all means that we aggregate wealth in each country over its inhabitants (to form the national stocks of wealth W and W^*) and allocate it to its four destinations. This further means we multiply the x-, x^*-, y-, y^*-, z-, z^*-, $1 - x - y - z$-, and $1 - x^* - y^* - z^*$- fractions with the national wealth levels. Expression (3.8) shows the resulting demand functions for the four assets.[11] The first term on the right-hand side indicates that in the trivial case where all four returns are equal (i. e., when the

---

[11] The aggregation also affects the interpretation of the θ-parameter and hence the ϕ_1-, ϕ_2-, ϕ_3-, and ϕ_4-parameters. The parameter of relative risk aversion depends on the wealth of the investor. Hence, the θ-parameter in the ϕ_1-, ϕ_2-, ϕ_3-, and ϕ_4-parameters of (3.8) is the wealth-weighted average of the individual θ-coefficients of a country ($\widehat{\theta}$ and $\widehat{\theta^*}$):

$$\widehat{\theta} = \sum_j \frac{\theta_j}{w_j/W} \text{ and } \widehat{\theta^*} = \sum_i \frac{\theta_i^*}{w_i/W^*} ,$$

(j and i index the investors of the two countries). In order to write (3.8) as indicated we assume that the two parameters $\widehat{\theta}$ and $\widehat{\theta^*}$ are the same in the two countries. The simplest case where this holds is when all individuals have equal wealth (i. e., when differing national wealth levels are merely a result of different population sizes).

second term on the right-hand side is zero) both countries' investors want to hold all their wealth in their own riskless asset.[12]

$$\begin{bmatrix} K_D \\ K_D^* \\ B_D \\ B_D^* \end{bmatrix} = \begin{bmatrix} 0 \\ 0 \\ W \\ W^* \end{bmatrix} + (W + W^*) \begin{bmatrix} \phi_1 & \phi_2 & -\phi_2 \\ -\phi_2 & -\phi_1 & \phi_1 \\ -\phi_1 & -\phi_4 & \phi_2 \\ \phi_2 & \phi_3 & -\phi_1 \end{bmatrix} \begin{bmatrix} (\bar{r} - i) \\ (i^* - i) \\ (\bar{r}^* - i) \end{bmatrix}$$

(3.8)

In the next step we specify the supplies of the four assets. Beginning with physical capital, I assume decreasing returns which implies that the marginal product of capital in a country is negatively related to the amount of capital invested in that country (K and K^*, respectively).[13] This means that there is a negative relationship between the return on capital in a country ($\bar{r}$ and $\bar{r}^*$) and the stock of capital in that country. The lower the expected return on capital required by the market the higher the stock of capital that is profitable in a country. This relationship is the supply function for physical capital.

To get a picture of the supply process of equity one can think of (unendowed) entrepreneurs who look at the expected return on capital they have to generate and then decide how much physical investment they want to realize. This capital stock is then financed by supplying equity to domestic and foreign wealth holders. To simplify matters we assume that the described capital supply relationship is linear and that the slope parameter ($\beta > 0$) is the same in both countries.

$$\begin{bmatrix} K_S \\ K_S^* \end{bmatrix} = \begin{bmatrix} \alpha \\ \alpha^* \end{bmatrix} - \beta \begin{bmatrix} \bar{r} \\ \bar{r}^* \end{bmatrix}$$

(3.9)

---

[12] Under fixed exchange rates the two bonds become perfect substitutes and the demand system is reduced to three equations. Going back to the setup of (3.5) it can be shown that the total demand for the generic type of bonds in this case is

$$B_D + B_D^* = W + W^* + (W + W^*)(-\phi_1 \quad \phi_2) \begin{bmatrix} (\bar{r} - i) \\ (\bar{r}^* - i) \end{bmatrix}$$

This is exactly what follows when the two bond demand functions in (3.8) are added under the condition that $i^* - i = 0$.

[13] This relationship between $\bar{r}$ and K results from a production function that contains as arguments, apart from capital, one or more fixed factors of production (like land and labor). See also appendix 3.B.

The country with the higher α is the one with the better investment possibilities. This means that this country can profitably employ a higher capital stock at any expected capital return.[14] This is detailed in appendix 3.B which also discusses the implications of country specific β-parameters (i. e., $\beta \neq \beta^*$) based on linearizations of Cobb-Douglas production functions. The only qualification for this case is that the role of the difference in the two α-parameters in the capital market equilibrium is attenuated compared to the situation where $\beta = \beta^*$.

Figure 3.1 shows the relationship expressed in (3.9) for one country. The capital stock is shown as a function of the expected equity yield. Clearly, the relationship depicted is the inverted curve of the marginal product of capital. Hence, for any given capital stock we can read from the horizontal axis the expected marginal product of capital (i. e., the expected return). This is tantamount to solving (3.9) for $\bar{r}$. The randomness of r can be visualized as productivity shocks which shift the depicted function to the right (positive shock) or the left (negative shock). The expected income of investors from the claims to a country's capital stock is indicated by the shaded rectangle. The shaded triangle is the expected income that goes to the other factors of

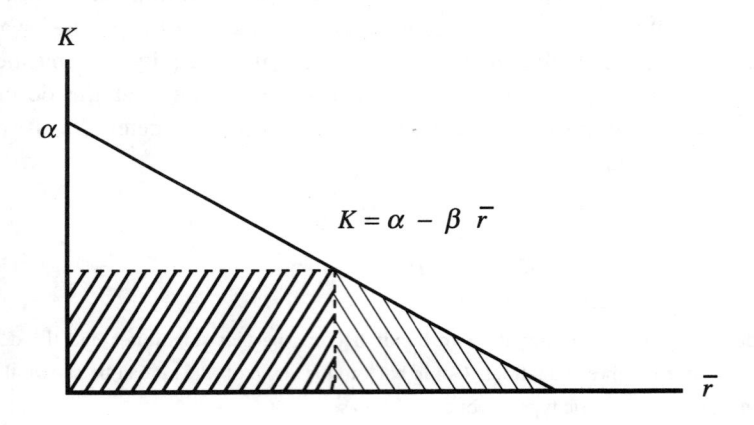

$$K = \alpha - \beta \bar{r}$$

Figure 3.1 *The Capital Stock as a Function of the Expected Marginal Product of Capital*

---

[14] It is assumed that the described capital supply functions are unaffected by the choice of exchange rate regime.

production (labor and land) assumed to be owned by residents of the country. Total expected output of the country concerned is the sum of the two shaded areas. These factor incomes will become important in the treatment of the politico-economic aspect of the choice of exchange rate regime.

The supply of bonds consists of obligations of the private sector. These are inside assets which means that their net supply is zero. Government bonds do not create a net supply of bonds because they are regarded by the public as implying future tax liabilities. Hence, claims on the government and liabilities to the government just cancel.[15] For our purposes the above is expressed as

$$\begin{bmatrix} B_S \\ B_S^* \end{bmatrix} = \begin{bmatrix} 0 \\ 0 \end{bmatrix} . \qquad (3.10)$$

The market for bonds of the private sector develops because the motive to hedge exchange rate risk on foreign equity investment induces people to supply bonds issued in the foreign currency and to demand bonds issued in their own currency. Since the foreigners have a reciprocal motivation they will generate a demand for bonds issued in their currency and a supply of bonds issued in the other currency. What has just been described naturally emerges from the mathematical formulation of the portfolio allocation problem since the portfolio fractions are not restricted to be non-negative. Typically, the fractions z and z^* will be negative. It is the cost of hedging (i. e., $i - i^*$) together with the returns on equity that brings demands in line with supplies in both countris' bond markets.[16] Obviously, if both countries were identical they would

---

[15] In other words, we do not consider government bonds as part of net wealth. See Barro (1974) for a formal proof of this proposition. Patinkin (1964, pp. 289-290) earlier suggested that the net supply of bonds is zero if the private sector correctly discounts its tax liability. Frankel (1979) discusses the role of government bonds in the determination of the foreign exchange risk premium in a model where purchasing power parity holds.

[16] If it turns out that country A wants a larger investment in country B's stocks than country B wants stock holdings in country A then the private bond supplies in country B will be larger than the bond supplies in country A. This will tendentially lead to a higher interest rate in country B. To put this another way, the residents of country A will pay a foreign exchange risk premium to hedge their foreign investment. Such a premium will deter some foreign equity investment and also induce the investors not to hedge all their currency risk. Both effects will reduce the supply of B-bonds. On the other hand, the residents of country B will get a kind of

generate perfectly reciprocal bond supplies and demands which in turn would result in identical interest rates in the two countries. It is clear that in this case hedging would be costless in both countries. Hence, all investors would fully hedge their currency risk on their foreign equity investments. In this case the choice of exchange rate regime would obviously have no impact on the capital market equilibrium.

The equilibrium conditions for the four asset markets can now be stated. After subtracting one of the two equity equilibrium conditions from the other (i. e., writing $K_D^* - K_D = K_S^* - K_S$) and rearranging equations we get a system of three simultaneous equations. The first equation is the combined expression of the two equity markets. The second equation captures equilibrium in the domestic bond market and the third equation describes equilibrium in the foreign bond market. Both sides of (3.11) have been divided by the term $W + W^*$.

$$\begin{bmatrix} -(\phi_1 + \phi_2 + \frac{\beta}{W+W^*}) & -(\phi_1 + \phi_2) & \phi_1 + \phi_2 + \frac{\beta}{W+W^*} \\ \phi_1 & \phi_4 & -\phi_2 \\ -\phi_2 & -\phi_3 & \phi_1 \end{bmatrix} \times \begin{bmatrix} (\bar{r} - i) \\ (i^* - i) \\ (\bar{r}^* - i) \end{bmatrix} = \begin{bmatrix} \frac{\alpha^* - \alpha}{W + W^*} \\ \frac{W}{W + W^*} \\ \frac{W^*}{W + W^*} \end{bmatrix} \quad (3.11)$$

The above equations determine the three return differentials: $\bar{r} - i$, $i^* - i$, and $\bar{r}^* - i$. For the subsequent discussion it is most useful to take the

---

subsidy on their foreign equity holdings. For every equity they buy in country A they can make a bond transaction (sell an A-bond and buy a B-bond) with a positive return. Naturally, this incentive has the tendency to increase the foreign investment of B-residents and it will also induce them to make bond transactions in excess of their foreign equity holdings. By doing the latter they take on some of the exchange rate risk that otherwise the A-residents would bear. Both effects increase the supply of A-bonds.

equilibrium conditions and rewrite them as equity return differentials and bond return differentials. In this form the results are:

$$\bar{r} - \bar{r}^* = \frac{\theta[\,2(1-\rho)\sigma_r^2 + \sigma_d^2](\alpha - \alpha^*) + \sigma_d^2 \theta(W^* - W)}{\beta\theta[2(1-\rho)\sigma_r^2 + \sigma_d^2] + 2(W^* + W)} \quad (3.12)$$

$$i - i^* = \frac{\sigma_d^2 \theta(\alpha - \alpha^*) + \dfrac{\sigma_d^2 \theta[(1-\rho)\beta\sigma_r^2 \theta + W^* + W]}{W^* + W}(W^* - W)}{\beta\theta[2(1-\rho)\sigma_r^2 + \sigma_d^2] + 2(W^* + W)} \quad (3.13)$$

In the above equations ρ stands for $\sigma_{r^*,r}/\sigma_r^2$, that is, the correlation between the two countries' equity returns. The terms to the left of $\alpha - \alpha^*$ and $W^* - W$ as well as the denominator of the two equations are strictly non-negative. The first point worth noting is that the relative equity and bond returns tend to be higher in the country with the better investment possibilities (i. e., $\alpha > \alpha^*$ tends to make $\bar{r} - \bar{r}^*$ and $i - i^*$ positive). The second observation is that the country with the larger wealth tends to have the lower yields (i. e., $W^* > W$ tends to make $\bar{r} - \bar{r}^*$ and $i - i^*$ positive).

The role of the exchange rate regime is readily visible in the two expressions above: with $\sigma_d^2 = 0$ the wealth term does not matter for $\bar{r} - \bar{r}^*$. In this case the difference in investment opportunities is the sole determinant of the difference in expected stock returns. Why is it that under a fixed exchange rate regime returns on capital can remain unequalized? The answer is to be found in the trade-off between return and risk: given a fixed exchange rate all investors hold the same all-equity portfolio. The optimal composition of this portfolio is the same for domestic and foreign investors. From the viewpoint of risk minimization an even composition, that is equal numbers of domestic and foreign stocks, would be optimal. However, unequal physical investment possibilities in the two countries mean that equal numbers of domestic and foreign stocks lead to a difference in returns. Hence, a diminution in the return difference means an internationally uneven portfolio: return equalization comes at the cost of increased risk. It is obvious that risk aversion determines - in a macroeconomic equilibrium - the extent of return equalization.

Under a fixed exchange rate the interest rate differential entirely vanishes. The latter result is straightforward because a fixed exchange rate turns the two bonds into perfect substitutes. Since the difference in bond returns is the foreign exchange risk premium it is also obvious that it has to vanish as the exchange rate risk vanishes.

3.3 The Effect of Floating the Exchange Rate

In this section we explore the model by discussing the consequences of moving from a fixed to a floating exchange rate (i. e., from $\sigma_d^2 = 0$ to $\sigma_d^2 > 0$). The primary effect that will be discussed is the impact of this regime change on the international distribution of capital. The capital stocks in the two countries are determined once the equity yield differential is determined. We know that the overall capital stock that can be allocated to the two countries is the sum of the two wealth levels:[17]

$$K + K^* = W + W^* \tag{3.14}$$

The difference in the two countries' capital stocks is:

$$K - K^* = (\alpha - \alpha^*) - \beta(\bar{r} - \bar{r}^*) \tag{3.15}$$

From the two above expressions the levels of the two capital stocks can be determined:

$$K = \frac{W + W^*}{2} + \frac{\alpha - \alpha^*}{2} - \frac{\beta}{2}(\bar{r} - \bar{r}^*) \tag{3.16}$$

and

$$K^* = \frac{W + W^*}{2} - \frac{\alpha - \alpha^*}{2} + \frac{\beta}{2}(\bar{r} - \bar{r}^*) \tag{3.17}$$

Hence, a change in the international allocation of capital can easily be assessed by looking at the change in the equity yield differential. If the equity return

---

[17] The real exchange rate at the beginning of the period (where all choices described happen) is standardized to one and investors cannot hold assets (e. g., land) other than those introduced in section 3.1.

differential narrows, for example, then a capital outflow from the formerly low capital return country to the high capital return country has occurred. In order to assess whether the capital return differential between the two countries widens or narrows or even reverses its sign with the move to a flexible exchange rate we look at (3.12). The following statements can be made:

1. In the case where both countries have equal wealth, the move to a flexible exchange rate widens the equity yield differential.[18] This is probably what intuition would tell us. The injection of an additional form of risk (exchange rate risk) necessitates a larger equity yield differential to motivate foreign investments. In the present case, the country with the higher equity yield under the fixed exchange rate experiences a capital outflow and a rise in its expected marginal product of capital. In contrast, the country with the lower capital return experiences an inflow of capital and a decrease in its return on capital.

2. When the country with the fewer investment possibilities (i. e., the country with the lower equity yield under the fixed exchange rate regime) has greater wealth the above outcome is amplified: The regime switch leads to an even larger inflow of capital into this country and a larger widening of the international equity yield differential.

3. If, however, the country with the fewer investment possibilities (i. e., the country with the lower equity return under the fixed exchange rate regime) is poorer than its neighbor then the regime switch can widen or narrow or possibly reverse the sign of the equity yield differential. Correspondingly, the direction of capital flows is ambiguous. The outcome depends on the physical investment opportunities, the wealth levels, the variance and the covariance of capital returns, the variance of the exchange rate, and the degree of risk aversion of investors. Hence, we can have the possibly counterintuitive outcome that the transition from a fixed to a flexible exchange rate leads to a convergence of equity yields.

---

[18] An increase in σ_d^2 raises the term to the left of $\alpha - \alpha^*$ proportionally more than it raises the denominator of (3.12).

4. In cases where $i - i^* = 0$ (i. e., when the foreign exchange risk premium is zero) hedging the exchange rate risk is free for all investors. Hence, the choice of exchange rate regime has no impact on the capital market equilibrium. Formally, this can be seen by extracting from (3.13) the condition under which $i - i^* = 0$:[19]

$$W^* - W = \frac{W^* + W}{(1 - \rho)\beta\sigma_r^2\theta + W^* + W}(\alpha^* - \alpha)$$

This means that the wealth difference needs to be the indicated proportion of the difference in investment opportunities. More specifically, under a floating exchange rate the country with the better investment opportunities has to have just the right wealth advantage to produce a situation where $i - i^* = 0$. The above expression represents for the present model what the various conditions derived in Frankel (1979) and Grinols and Turnovsky (1991) represent for their models: it shows under which circumstances exchange rate risk is fully diversifiable. If the above condition is inserted into (3.12) the equity yield differential under $i - i^* = 0$ can be determined. It turns out that it is:

$$\bar{r} - \bar{r}^* = \frac{\theta(1 - \rho)\sigma_r^2}{\beta\theta(1 - \rho)\sigma_r^2 + W^* + W}(\alpha - \alpha^*)$$

This expression makes clear that with a zero foreign exchange risk premium the equity yield differential and hence the allocation of physical capital to the two countries does not depend on σ_d^2.

In the following the effect of floating the currencies is analyzed in greater detail. Here, the question is asked how a gradual increase in the variance of the exchange rate affects the equity return differential and the interest rate differential. One of the interesting results is that the two yield differentials are not necessarily of the same sign. The condition derived under point 4 above turns out to be useful in displaying the relationships derived. The discussion will be conducted by means of several figures.

---

[19] Note that the following condition does not depend on the variance of the exchange rate.

Figure 3.2 displays the equity return differential $\bar{r} - \bar{r}^*$ in the case where the domestic country has the superior physical investment opportunities (i. e., $\alpha > \alpha^*$). In this case the equity yield differential is positive under a fixed exchange rate (i. e., when $\sigma_d^2 = 0$). As σ_d^2 starts to rise the direction in which $\bar{r} - \bar{r}^*$ changes depends on the size of the wealth differential relative to the difference in investment opportunities. Each of the straight lines displays a linear approximation of the response of $\bar{r} - \bar{r}^*$ to changes in σ_d^2 for a given combination of wealth levels and investment opportunities. In the case where the relative size of these terms is the size derived under point 4 above (where $i - i^* = 0$ results) the equity return differential does not change with σ_d^2. This case is indicated by the fat horizontal line in figure 3.2. When the domestic net wealth is lower (higher) than the critical value just mentioned, an increase in σ_d^2 certainly leads to an increase (decrease) in the equity yield differential. The thin arrow indicates how the outcome in terms of equity return differential changes as the size of W is increased relative to the size of W^*.

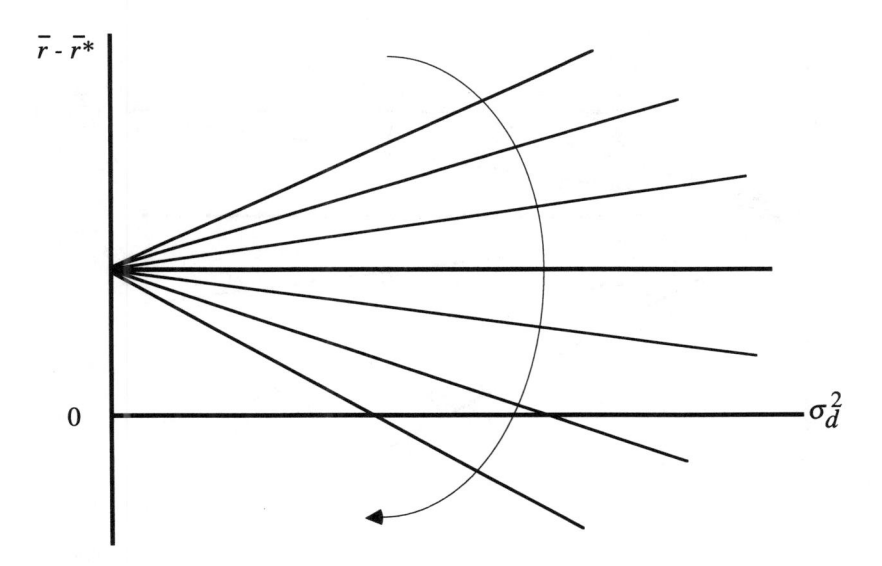

Figure 3.2 *The Equity Return Differential as a Function of the Variance of the Exchange Rate for the Case where the Domestic Country has the Superior Investment Opportunities*

Figure 3.2 also complements and sharpens the statements 1, 2, and 3. It shows that, if the domestic wealth is above a certain threshold, a large enough increase in σ_d^2 will reverse the sign of the equity yield differential. Hence, there are cases where it is not possible to say whether floating currencies will produce an equity yield differential in favor of the home or the foreign country without knowing the magnitude of the exchange rate fluctuations.

Figure 3.3 displays the same relationship for the case where $\alpha < \alpha^*$. This is the opposite case to the one depicted in figure 3.2: here, the foreign country has the better physical investment opportunities. In this case the outcome under a fixed exchange rate is a lower equity yield in the home country compared to the return in the foreign country. The thin arrow again indicates how the outcome changes with higher levels of W. When the domestic net wealth is higher than the threshold that produces $i - i^* = 0$, an increase in σ_d^2 certainly lowers the domestic equity yield.

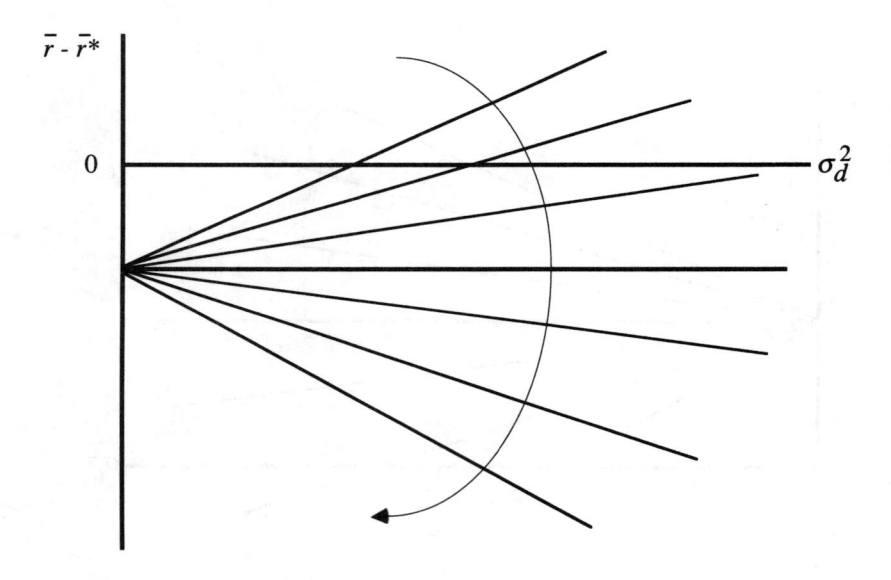

Figure 3.3 *The Equity Return Differential as a Function of the Variance of the Exchange Rate for the Case where the Foreign Country has the Superior Investment Opportunities*

Figure 3.4 shows the interest rate differential $i - i^*$. It is clear from (3.13) that this yield differential is zero when σ_d^2 is zero. The solid horizontal line coinciding with the axis displays the case where $\alpha - \alpha^*$ and $W - W^*$ have their relative size derived under point 4 above. This is the case where $i - i^*$ is zero no matter what value σ_d^2 takes. Again, the thin arrow indicates how the outcome changes with higher levels of domestic wealth. When figures 3.2, 3.3, and 3.4 are taken together it becomes clear that the equity yield differential and the interest rate differential do not have to be of the same sign. The important point is, however, that the sign of an emerging interest rate differential indicates which country will experience a decline in its equity return. If the wealth levels and investment opportunities are such that we move along one of the downward sloping lines in figure 3.4 as σ_d^2 increases, we will also move along one of the downward sloping lines in figures 3.2 or 3.3. Hence, the following simple and general rule holds. The country that emerges under flexible exchange rates as the one with the lower bond return will also be the one that experiences a capital inflow and a drop in the marginal product of capital. Thus, this is a case where a general equilibrium outcome contradicts the notion that capital flows in the direction of the higher interest rate.

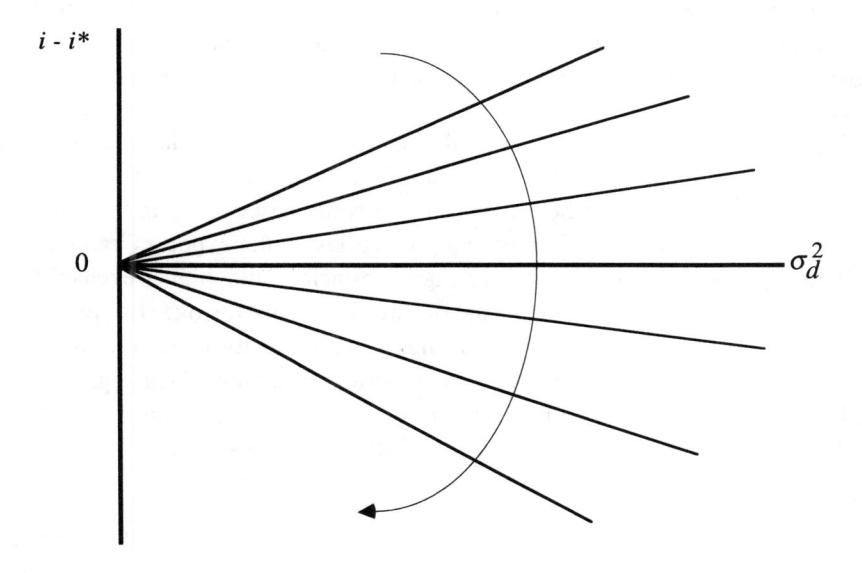

Figure 3.4 *The Interest Rate Differential as a Function of the Variance of the Exchange Rate*

3.4 The Feldstein-Horioka Puzzle

Feldstein and Horioka (1980) documented the fact that in national economies investment and savings strongly co-move. The two authors document this by means of a cross-sectional regression relating the ratio of gross domestic investment to gross domestic product to the ratio of gross national savings to gross domestic product:

$$\left(\frac{I}{Y}\right)_i = \alpha + \beta \left(\frac{S}{Y}\right)_i$$

The variables are data averages for countries over several years and i is the country index.[20] Perfect capital mobility, according to Feldstein and Horioka, would imply an estimate of β close to zero. If capital were to flow easily to the most profitable location then an increase in national savings would very likely be allocated abroad. The effect on the domestic capital stock should be about proportional to the size of the domestic capital stock relative to the world capital stock. In fact the estimated β turns out to be significantly larger than zero and in some cases not significantly different from one. This means that investment has a home bias: savings tend to remain in the economy that generates them. The reported finding has stood up to further scrutiny by a number of other researchers although the estimates of β in later studies are smaller.[21]

The present analysis suggests that the reported empirical finding may be due to exchange rate risk.[22] The interpretation of the history of the Feldstein-Horioka regularity suggested here is that, while some obstacles to the international dispersion of savings - like official restrictions on the export of capital - have largely disappeared in recent years, new obstacles - like higher exchange rate risk - have appeared. The basis of the Feldstein-Horioka finding is asymmetric wealth accumulation. If savings were perfectly correlated there would be no point in estimating a Feldstein-Horioka equation. Their regressor would have no variance. The two authors detail the variations in domestic saving rates among the countries in the introduction to their study.

---

[20] In the base regression the averages are over 14 years. The finding is also present when the regression is run with five year averages.
[21] See, e. g., Dooley et al. (1987) and Tesar (1991).
[22] This view is shared by Frankel (1991).

In order to assess whether unequal additions to wealth produce the reported dependence of investment on domestic savings I use my model to analyze a situation where there is a wealth addition in just one of the two countries. The two countries in the experiment have identical investment opportunities (i. e., $\alpha = \alpha^*$) and initially identical net wealth levels (i. e., $W^* = W$). This means there are identical capital stocks and identical equity yields in both countries. Under a fixed exchange rate, additional savings (dW) will not affect $\bar{r} - \bar{r}^*$ and will be equally distributed over the two countries' capital stocks. This means

$$\frac{dK}{dW}_{Fix} = \frac{1}{2}. \qquad (3.18)$$

Hence, under a fixed exchange rate the domestic capital stock is indeed increased proportionally to its size relative to the world capital stock. Under a flexible exchange rate the equity return differential is also zero at the beginning. However, the increase dW lowers $\bar{r}$ relative to $\bar{r}^*$. This implies that with exchange rate risk a larger fraction of the additional savings is allocated to the domestic capital stock:

$$\frac{dK}{dW}_{Flex} = \frac{1}{2} - \frac{\beta}{2} \frac{d(\bar{r} - \bar{r}^*)}{dW} > \frac{dK}{dW}_{Fix} \qquad (3.19)$$

The above result indicates that flexible exchange rates are partly responsible for the home bias in investment observed even in recent years.

3.5 Exchange Rate Regime and Net Foreign Asset Position

It is interesting to note what can happen to the net foreign wealth of a country. The net foreign asset position of the home economy is

$$A = yW + zW - y^*W^* - z^*W^*. \qquad (3.20)$$

Expressions for y and y^* can be deduced from the capital market equilibrium conditions. From $xW + y^*W^* = K$ follows (since $x = y^*$)

$$y^* = \frac{K}{W + W^*}. \qquad (3.21)$$

Similarly, from $yW + x^*W^* = K^*$ follows (since $x^* = y$)

$$y = \frac{K^*}{W + W^*}.\qquad(3.22)$$

Next, we seek an expression for the fraction z. We know from section 3.1 that the fraction of foreign bonds the foreign investor wants to hold (i. e., $1 - x^* - y^* - z^*$) is equal to one plus the fraction the domestic investor wants to hold in the same type of asset (i. e., $1 + z$). Hence, we can write the equilibrium condition for the foreign bond market as:

$$zW + (1 + z)W^* = 0 \qquad(3.23)$$

This leads to

$$z = -\frac{W^*}{W + W^*}.\qquad(3.24)$$

The corresponding expression for z^* is:

$$z^* = -\frac{W}{W + W^*}\qquad(3.25)$$

Using the above expressions, A can be expressed as[23]

$$A = \frac{WK^* - W^*K}{W + W^*}.\qquad(3.26)$$

It becomes clear from this expression that the net foreign asset position is influenced by the allocation of physical capital to the two countries (K and K^*). This means that A is potentially affected by the choice of exchange rate regime. Imagine, for example, a situation where the home country has inferior investment possibilities (i. e., $\alpha < \alpha^*$). In this case a fixed exchange rate certainly means that K^* is larger than K. In a case where $W > W^*$, a positive net foreign asset position of the home country is a certain outcome. The move to a flexible exchange rate can tilt this situation. The wealth differential now

---

[23] The terms involving z and z^* cancel out, true to the proposition that for both countries bond debts abroad exactly match bond credits at home.

leads to an increase in K and a decrease in K^*. If this effect is strong enough A turns negative. Therefore, it can happen that a country that was a net creditor under a fixed exchange rate becomes a net debtor under floating currencies.

3.6 Considerations of Efficiency and Political Economy

This section looks at the effect on efficiency of the regime choice. It has to be pointed out that the propositions outlined here are tentative. This is due to several reasons: first, this study has not developed an explanation of exchange rate variability. Hence, I cannot say what level of exchange rate variability is induced by a specific type of monetary policy, like inflation targeting. Second, fixing the exchange rate may generate variability in other variables (e. g., interest rates). Such compensatory variability, although potentially interesting, is not captured in the model developed in this chapter. Third, the proposition that a flexible exchange rate may be efficiency improving does not hold for all levels of exchange rate variance but only for a specific, optimal level. This ties in with the first point: nothing is said here about how this optimal level of exchange rate variability can be achieved.

For expositional reasons I start by looking at the interests of the various actors involved (investors and land owners and labor) without distinguishing, for the moment, any differences in residence. This approach - putting a veil over the national identity of resource owners - allows a clearer discussion of the overall efficiency issues. It is clear that portfolio variance rises with the transition from a fixed to a flexible exchange rate.[24] In this respect, floating the exchange rate tends to lower investors' welfare. Therefore, investors will prefer fixed over flexible exchange rates. The preference of investors can, however, be at odds with the interests of the owners of the other factors of production. The decision where to allocate the savings also affects production in the two countries. The sum of the two expected outputs is maximized when the marginal products of capital in the two countries are equalized.[25]

---

[24] Except in the case where $i - i^* = 0$, that is, when the foreign asset positions of both countries are fully hedged. It is assumed that $\sigma_{r^*, r}$ and σ_r^2 remain unchanged.

[25] See figure 3.1 for the measurement of expected output. The situation where the equity yield differential is minimal is not necessarily also the one where expected output is at its maximum. A given absolute capital return differential is always associated with a higher sum of the two expected outputs when the capital return differential is in favor of the country with the better

It will now be shown in detail that the amount of exchange rate risk - hence the exchange rate regime - that maximizes investors' utility is not necessarily the one that maximizes expected output in this two-country world. In order to do this we go back to the situation described in figure 3.3: the domestic country has the lower capital return under a fixed exchange rate. This can occur when the domestic economy is the one with the fewer physical investment possibilities. There are basically two cases to be considered here. Figure 3.5 shows these two cases. The first (second) case is the one where the domestic country's wealth is larger (smaller) than the critical level described on page 54. In this first case an increase in exchange rate risk (i. e., in $\sigma_{\tilde{q}}^2$) will lead to a widening of the return gap between the two countries. This coincides with a decrease in the expected output of the two-country world. The optimal exchange rate regime, from the viewpoint of output maximization, is thus the fixed exchange rate regime. Here, this choice also maximizes investor's utility because it minimizes portfolio variance. Under the present conditions and from the perspective of output maximization a positive level of exchange rate risk would lead to an over-allocation of wealth to the domestic economy.

In the second case, where domestic wealth is below the critical level, exchange rate risk deters more foreign investment than it induces extra domestic investment. The result in this case is that the equity return differential narrows. This implies that the amount of exchange rate risk that maximizes expected output is not the same as the amount maximizing investor's utility. The reason for this can be described as follows: investors' tendency to diversify wealth implies an over-allocation of wealth to the economy where capital is less productive. In other words: an investor's decisions to allocate wealth has an externality with respect to the productivity of the other factors involved in production (land and labor). This externality may lead to an allocation of wealth which is at odds with the interests of land and labor. Owners of land and

---

investment opportunities. Hence, it can happen that a regime switch is output increasing even when the absolute capital return differential widens.

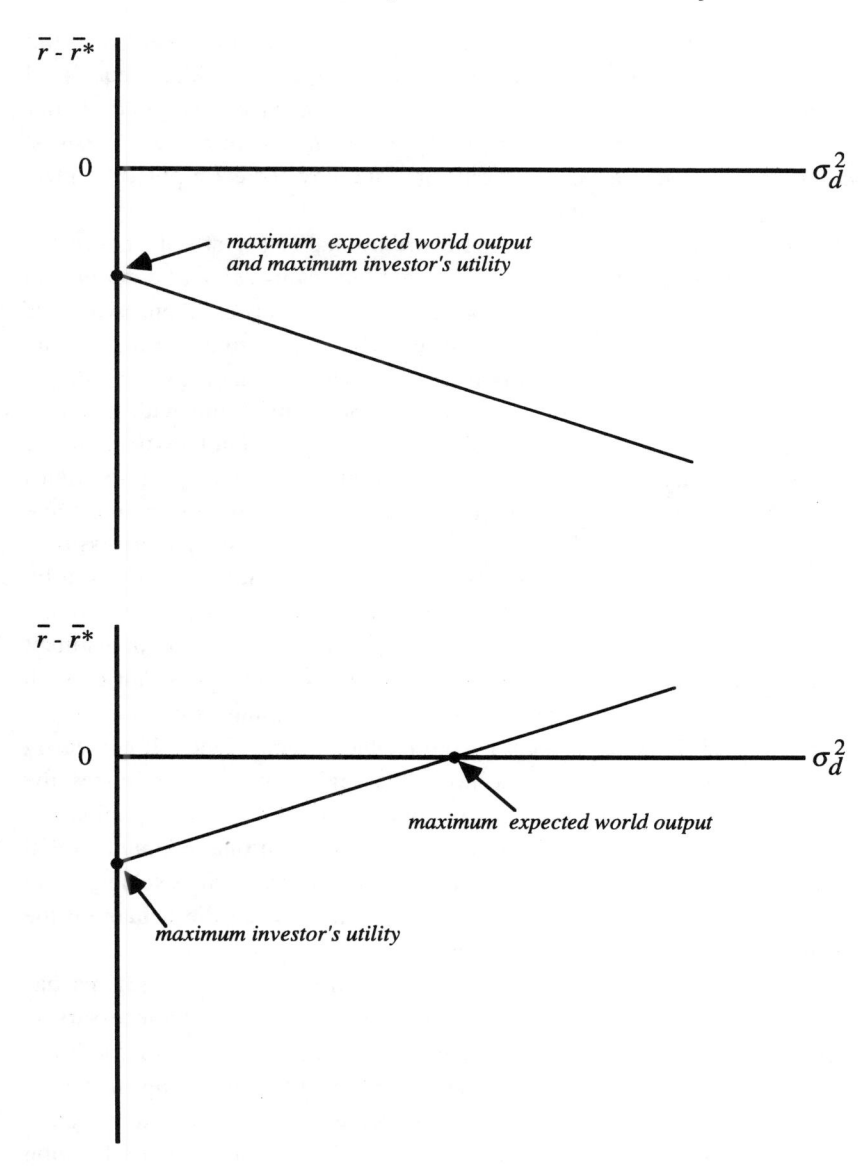

Figure 3.5 *Optimal Variance of the Exchange Rate with Respect to Expected World Output and Investor's Utility in Two Possible Cases*

labor would prefer a flexible exchange rate if this flexibility were to bring about a level of exchange rate variance close to the one that produces equalized capital returns. Adopting a flexible exchange rate can make everybody better off if part of the income gain of land and labor is transferred to investors. Hence, in specific cases a flexible exchange rate may correct a possible international misallocation of savings.[26]

These considerations indicate that distributional issues are of importance in the choice of a monetary regime. If productivity gains cannot be divided so as to make an efficient outcome advantageous to all parties, then owners of different resources may have diverging views with respect to the exchange rate regime they favor. This is particularly obvious when we consider the diverging interests of the owners of the same type of resource but with different residency. Generally, it can be said that workers and land owners in the country experiencing a capital inflow (concurrent with a falling equity yield) with the transition to a different exchange rate regime will see their income rise. In the other country workers and land owners will lose. The assessment of investors, once we consider their residence, is not simply tied to portfolio variance: the level of the expected return on their savings is affected by the regime choice, too. Investors of the country with the superior investment possibilities have no interest in sharing these investment opportunities with foreign investors if the advantage of high domestic capital returns outweighs the gain from risk reduction under a fixed exchange rate. Hence, it can easily happen that investors in a country favor the regime which maximizes the equity yield in their country, which is the one that minimizes its capital stock. Therefore, within any country labor and land owners on one side and capital on the other side may take opposing views with respect to the exchange rate regime preferred. This type of conflict is well known from the debate on the liberalization of international capital flows.[27]

This discussion shows that the choice of an exchange rate regime has many distributional implications. Some of the transfer payments necessary to gain widespread support for an efficient regime involve schemes for international transfers. Hence, a transnational structure like the European Union may be helpful to their members when it comes to choosing the efficient exchange rate regime. From the viewpoint of optimal international allocation

---

[26] Other actions, like taxation of capital returns, may represent possibly superior alternative policy measures to correct for this externality.

[27] See MacDougall (1960).

of savings there is one further issue, though: the same regime should not be applied everywhere. It can be argued that economies which are relatively poor and have scarce physical investment possibilities ought to be tied to the rest of the economic community by flexible exchange rates. Why should this be so? Funds in search of international diversification may over-allocate savings to these economies. Flexible exchange rates will limit this tendency.

Next, we abstract from the possibility of welfare improving transfer payments. In this case - in a democracy - the majority of votes in a country determines the choice of the exchange rate regime in that country. In order to have an idea whether the exchange rate between any two countries is fixed or flexible one has to ask first which regime would be adopted should the two countries disagree. One view would have it that in this case a fixed exchange rate is the outcome because a country cannot prevent another country from pegging its currency. If this is the case, then a flexible exchange rate would be the exception. Another view would have it that a regime of fixed exchange rates needs coordination and that, in the absence of a consensus between countries, a floating of currencies results. If this is the case, then obviously a fixed exchange rate would be the exception. The second question is, of course, which exchange rate regime has the approval of the majority of the population. In general the answer depends on the political coalitions formed between owners of different factors of production, on the size of their endowments, and the investment possibilities of a country. Specific answers are hard to come by, though. Instead, an example has to suffice: floating currencies may be the result when the rich country has poor investment opportunities and is ruled by a coalition of labor and land owners while the other country is ruled by a government favoring the interests of capital. The exchange rate risk would in this case prevent some capital from flowing out of the rich country. This would keep wages and rents high in the rich country while keeping the return on capital high in the other country. This seems like a fairly unstable equilibrium. Any change in political power can lead to a switch in the exchange rate regime. This introduces a further - political - risk. The implied regime volatility is hardly in anyone's long-run interest and the analysis of its effects goes beyond this study.

3.7 Conclusions

The implications of this two-country model can be summed up as follows: The move from a fixed to a flexible exchange rate is likely to change the international distribution of physical capital. This happens because the regime of flexible exchange rates, except under special conditions, induces a difference in bond returns between countries. This interest rate differential makes investment in equity in the country with the lower bond return more attractive to both foreign and domestic investors. The foreign investor can hedge her currency risk on this investment and make an additional net return on her hedging transactions. The domestic investor, however, sees his return on the domestic equity increased relative to the foreign equity because he has to pay a positive premium if he wants to hedge the exchange rate risk on his foreign investment. Hence, the country with the lower interest rate (determined by the interactions of all asset markets) will also be the one experiencing a capital inflow after the transition to floating currencies. Which country ends up in this situation depends on the physical investment opportunities, the wealth levels, the variance and the covariance of capital returns, the variance of the exchange rate, and on the degree of risk aversion of investors.

If the international distribution of capital differs under fixed and under flexible exchange rates, the choice of exchange rate regime will affect the productivity of total wealth and global welfare. These changes in productivity will affect owners of various factors of production in different ways. Thus, the choice of regime depends also on the existing schemes for distributing welfare gains.

Appendix 3.A: Derivation of the Mean-Variance Utility Function

This appendix demonstrates the derivation of a utility function $[U = U(\overline{w}, \sigma_{\widetilde{w}}^2)$, equation (3.1)] with the expected end-of-period wealth and the variance of end-of-period wealth as arguments from expected utility maximization with an underlying quadratic utility function $u = a\widetilde{w} - b\widetilde{w}^2$ ($\widetilde{w}$ is end-of-period wealth which is equal to consumption). We start by writing expected utility:

$$E\, u(\widetilde{w}) = E(a\widetilde{w} - b\widetilde{w}^2) = aE(\widetilde{w}) - bE(\widetilde{w}^2) \tag{A3.1}$$

Given that for any X and Y

$$E(XY) = E(X)E(Y) + \sigma_{X,Y} \tag{A3.2}$$

$E(\widetilde{w}^2)$ can be rewritten as

$$E(\widetilde{w}^2) = \overline{w}^2 + \sigma_{\widetilde{w}}^2 . \tag{A3.3}$$

As in the main text $\overline{w}$ denotes expected end-of-period wealth and $\sigma_{\widetilde{w}}^2$ denotes the variance of end-of-period wealth. If (A3.3) is inserted into (A3.1) the following expression can be written as the explicit form of the utility function in (3.1):

$$E\, u(\widetilde{w}) = a\overline{w} - b\overline{w}^2 - b\sigma_{\widetilde{w}}^2 = U(\overline{w}, \sigma_{\widetilde{w}}^2) \tag{A3.4}$$

It can also be shown how the parameter of relative risk aversion relates to the above utility function. The Pratt (1964) measure of relative risk aversion is

$$\delta = -\frac{u''\widetilde{w}}{u'} = -\frac{-2b\widetilde{w}}{a - 2b\widetilde{w}} . \tag{A3.5}$$

This is the same expression as the measure of relative risk aversion used in the text with the exception that w and $\overline{w}$ take the place of $\widetilde{w}$:

$$\theta = -\frac{2U_2 w}{U_1} = -\frac{-2bw}{a - 2b\overline{w}} . \tag{A3.6}$$

Appendix 3.B: The Effect of Unequal β-Parameters

This appendix generalizes the result obtained in (3.12) and (3.13) when the two countries do not have the same β-parameter. This happens when the linear capital supply functions in (3.9) are seen as linear approximations of supply functions based on Cobb-Douglas production functions. Setting the first derivative of output with respect to the capital stock equal to the expected capital return the capital stock can be written as

$$K = \left[\frac{1-v}{\hat{r}}\right]^{\frac{1}{v}} L \quad . \tag{B3.1}$$

L indicates a fixed factor of production (like labor or land). The parameter v denotes L's share in aggregate income. (B3.1) says that the capital stock, at any given level of capital return, is higher the higher L is. Hence, we identify the country with the higher L as the one with the better investment opportunities. We can pick an arbitrary positive capital return $\hat{r}$, calculate the two K-values that correspond to the two levels of L-input (the domestic level L and the foreign level L^*) and thus reach parameters that correspond to the α and α^* of the expression (3.9):

$$\alpha = \left[\frac{1-v}{\hat{r}}\right]^{\frac{1}{v}} L \text{ and } \alpha^* = \left[\frac{1-v}{\hat{r}}\right]^{\frac{1}{v}} L^* \tag{B3.2}$$

The slope corresponding to β from the Cobb-Douglas function is

$$\frac{\partial K}{\partial \hat{r}} = - \frac{(1-v)^{\frac{1}{v}}}{v \hat{r}^{\frac{v+1}{v}}} L \quad . \tag{B3.3}$$

This expression says that the country with the better investment possibilities (the one with the higher L) is also the one with the higher β-slope. Figure 3.B1 shows the two features developed in (B3.2) and (B3.3).

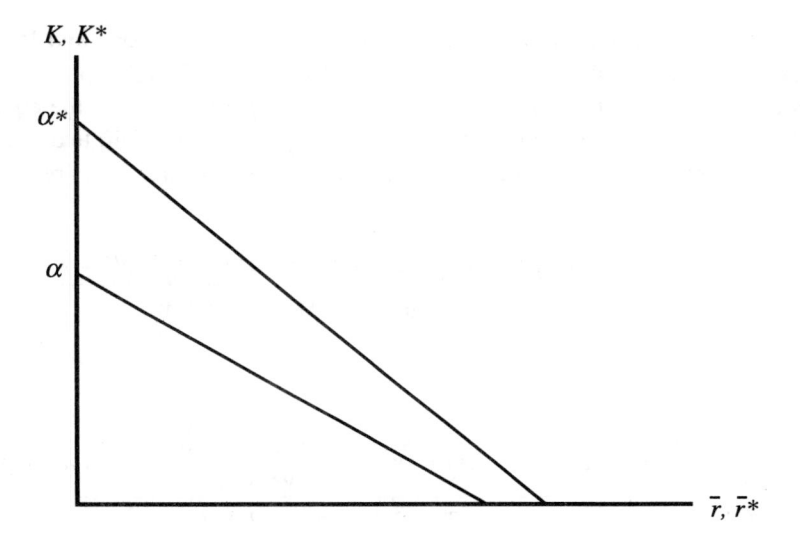

Figure 3.B1 *The Linearized Capital Supply Functions Based on a Cobb-Douglas Production Function*

The relationship between the α- and β-parameters developed above can be expressed by the following relationship:

$$\beta^* = \beta + \vartheta(\alpha^* - \alpha) \quad \text{with} \quad \frac{1}{\bar{r}^*} > \vartheta > 0 \ . \tag{B3.4}$$

The restriction $1/\bar{r}^* > \vartheta$ guarantees that the country with the higher α is always the one with the higher K at any given capital return. This is illustrated in figure 3.B1. Based on these formulations we can derive the new capital market equilibrium condition. The difference $K_S^* - K_S$ that leads up to the first line in expression (3.11) is new

$$K_S^* - K_S = (1 - \vartheta \bar{r}^*)(\alpha^* - \alpha) - \beta(\bar{r}^* - \bar{r})$$

instead of $K_S^* - K_S = (\alpha^* - \alpha) - \beta(\bar{r}^* - \bar{r})$.

Hence, the only thing that changes in the resulting equilibrium returns is that the term $\alpha - \alpha^*$ in (3.12) and (3.13) is multiplied by the term $1 - \vartheta \bar{r}^*$. From

(B3.4) it is known that the latter term is always smaller than one and larger than zero. Hence, with β-parameters derived from Cobb-Douglas production functions, the effect of the difference in investment opportunities on the equity yield differential is in general smaller than in the case in the main text where $\beta = \beta^*$. The equilibrium yield differentials for the more general case are:

$$\overline{r} - \overline{r}^*\bigg|_{\beta \neq \beta^*} = \frac{\theta[\,2(1-\rho)\sigma_r^2 + \sigma_d^2](1 - \vartheta \overline{r}^*)(\alpha - \alpha^*) + \sigma_d^2 \theta(W^* - W)}{\beta \theta[2(1-\rho)\sigma_r^2 + \sigma_d^2] + 2(W^* + W)}$$

(B3.5)

$$i - i^*\bigg|_{\beta \neq \beta^*} = \frac{\sigma_d^2 \theta(1 - \vartheta \overline{r}^*)(\alpha - \alpha^*) + \dfrac{\sigma_d^2 \theta[(1-\rho)\beta \sigma_r^2 \theta + W^* + W]}{W^* + W}(W^* - W)}{\beta \theta[2(1-\rho)\sigma_r^2 + \sigma_d^2] + 2(W^* + W)}$$

(B3.6)

Hauptsachen
wünsche ich an folgende Adresse:

Name: _____

Vorname: _____

Strasse: _____

PLZ, Ort _____

Damit wir Sie regelmässig mit Informationen bedienen können, erlauben wir uns, Ihre Angaben elektronisch zu speichern.

Verlag Paul Haupt
Falkenplatz 14
CH-3001 Bern

Bitte
frankieren

Liebe Leserin, lieber Leser

gerne informieren wir Sie regelmässig über unsere Neuerscheinungen.
Bitte kreuzen Sie Ihre Interessensgebiete an und senden diese Karte an uns zurück.

Hauptsachen:

- ☐ Sozialarbeit
- ☐ Betriebswirtschaft
- ☐ Pädagogik
- ☐ Bank- und Finanzwirtschaft
- ☐ Heil- und Sonderpädagogik
- ☐ Wirtschaftsethik
- ☐ Germanistik
- ☐ Volkswirtschaft
- ☐ Philosophie
- ☐ Recht
- ☐ Musikwissenschaft
- ☐ Politik
- ☐ Textiles
- ☐ Ökologie / Forstwesen
- ☐ Werken und Gestalten
- ☐ _____
- ☐ Schweizer Heimatbücher/ Volkskundliches

1/95

Verlag Paul Haupt Bern · Stuttgart · Wien

4

An Empirical Investigation on Exchange Rate Regimes and Capital Accumulation: Switzerland 1950-1990

The present empirical investigation addresses the question of how the transition from fixed to flexible exchange rates affects capital accumulation in a small open economy. Chapter 3 provides the theoretical background for this endeavor. The essence of chapter 3 can be summarized as follows: Flexible exchange rates add a new type of risk to foreign investment. Investors can hedge the exchange rate risk on their foreign investment by selling their proceeds on the forward exchange market or by holding a bond debt denominated in the foreign currency. However, such hedging is costly for the investor for whom the market determines a positive risk premium on his country's currency. This risk premium is positive - looking at a case where the expected change in the exchange rate is zero - if the foreign interest rate is higher than the domestic interest rate.[1] Hence, for the investor who experiences the emergence of a positive risk premium (i. e., a lower domestic interest rate) concomitant with the transition to floating currencies investments abroad become less attractive. As a result he will want to hold a larger portion of his wealth in domestic equities. For the investor of the country with the higher interest rate equity investment across the border also becomes more interesting. She will be able to engage in bond or forward exchange transactions that will hedge the currency risk on her investment abroad while also paying a positive net return. Both domestic and foreign investors are thus compelled to shift equity investment to the country that emerges as the low interest rate

---

[1] For an empirical measurement of the cost of hedging the expected change in the exchange rate has to be taken into account. See the reference to Frankel and MacArthur (1988) later in this text.

country under floating currencies. As a result, the capital stock in that country rises with the transition from fixed to flexible exchange rates.

The theoretical analysis in section 3.3 indicated that the inflow of capital after the transition to flexible exchange rates is likely to happen to a country with relatively large wealth and comparatively meager physical investment possibilities. Switzerland fits this description. It has been amply documented that the Swiss real interest rate under the regime of floating exchange rates has been substantially lower than, for example, the U. S. real interest rate.[2] Provided that covered interest rate parity holds the real interest rate differential consists of the foreign exchange risk premium - the cost of hedging exchange rate risk which is the variable of interest here - and the expected change in the real exchange rate. Frankel and MacArthur (1988) decompose the real interest rate differential into these two components and find that there is a substantial foreign exchange risk premium on the Swiss franc (i. e., on the forward exchange market the Swiss franc costs more than its expected value). One would expect from this that the transition from fixed to flexible exchange rates has led to an increase in the Swiss capital stock because the emergence of a positive foreign exchange risk premium has made investment in Swiss physical capital more attractive to domestic and foreign investors. The purpose of this chapter is to investigate whether the historical data are in accordance with this proposition.

The theoretical analysis of chapter 3 assumed unchanged levels of wealth. We continue to work with this assumption because the reallocation of given levels of wealth in response to a regime switch is judged to be quantitatively more important than the induced changes in savings. Chapter 2 showed that savings under flexible exchange rates can be either higher or lower than under fixed exchange rates depending on what rules and procedures central banks follow.[3]

---

[2] See, e. g., Frankel (1991).

[3] Clearly, once changes in wealth become quantitatively important influences on savings other than the influence of the monetary regime also enter the picture.

4.1 The Historical Background

Switzerland has had two distinctively different monetary regimes in the post-war period. Until 1973, the Swiss franc, like most currencies, was pegged to the dollar. Since 1973 the Swiss franc has been floating and the Swiss National Bank has pursued a policy of money stock targeting geared to keeping inflation in check. Unlike many other European countries, Switzerland has not become part of the European Monetary System. These policy choices have led to substantial exchange rate variations over the entire period of floating. This holds for the exchange rate of the Swiss franc relative to the U. S. dollar as well as to the German mark.

Figure 4.1 shows monthly observations of the franc-dollar exchange rate. The figure indicates that up to the beginning of the 1970s the exchange rate of the Swiss franc was pegged to the dollar. In the period before 1971 the variations in the value of the Swiss currency were minimal. In 1971, the erosion of the dollar's value began which ultimately led to the franc's free float in 1973. Figure 4.2 shows a measure of the exchange rate variability based on monthly observations. The measure depicted is the standard deviation of the monthly observations of the exchange rate. The plotted series indicates that the exact time of the transition to flexible exchange rates is not clear. Officially, the policy of pegging the Swiss franc to the dollar was not abandoned until 1973. However, the exchange rate revaluations of the two-year period before clearly injected exchange rate uncertainty into the system. The figure indicates that the decisive change in uncertainty occurred in 1971. Hence, the year 1971 will from now on be referred to as the year of the regime switch.[4]

In the next section I attempt to estimate quantitatively the effect of the switch in exchange rate regime on capital accumulation. This is done by way of econometric estimates of an investment equation. An alternative would be to base comparisons on ratios of real income to the capital stock. Multiplying this

---

[4] A word of caution is in order here. Even in the simple two-country portfolio-allocation framework presented in chapter 3 the international wealth allocation is influenced by the covariance between the returns on investment in the two countries. Technological changes may induce changes in the correlation between the returns on investment and may thus also affect the capital market equilibrium. If this effect is of historical importance the quality of the estimates in this chapter is diminished.

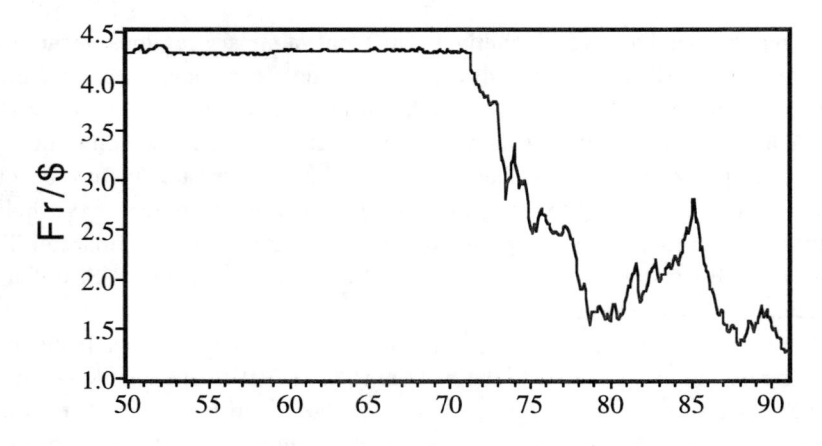

Figure 4.1 *The Franc-Dollar Exchange Rate*

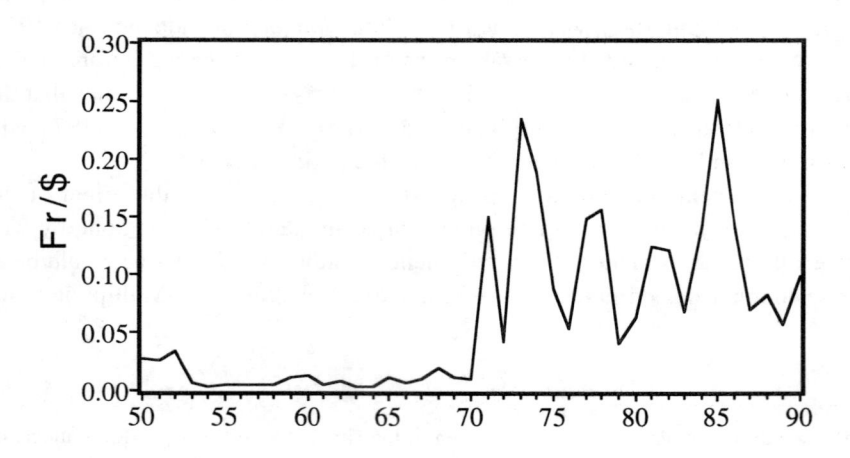

Figure 4.2 *The Standard Deviation of the Franc-Dollar Exchange Rate*

ratio by the elasticity of output with respect to the capital stock gives an estimate of the marginal product of capital. An estimate of the effect of exchange rate risk on the capital stock could then be arrived at by calculating the change in the capital stock necessary to generate the difference in the marginal product between the two exchange rate regimes. Among the many difficulties that affect this approach the most important is probably that a measure of the capital stock has to be used. Unfortunately, there are many sources of errors that can make measures of the capital stock unreliable.[5] It is the advantage of investment equations that they can be estimated without using any measure of the capital stock.

4.2 Estimating the Effect on Capital Accumulation

A large number of empirical studies on investment behavior has been cast in the mould of the accelerator model of investment. Clark (1979) provides a good survey of the various versions of the accelerator model and its competitors as well as estimates of these models for the United States. Bernanke, Bohn, and Reiss (1988), in a more recent study, confirm that the accelerator model is still one of the best models available for empirical work.[6] The accelerator model is firmly built on the assumption of optimizing agents as Fair (1984) points out. The basic idea is that optimization and competition determine an equilibrium capital stock (K^*) where the marginal product of capital is equal to the return that can be gained on an alternative investment with the same risk

---

[5] Capital stock series are typically calculated based on the assumption that a constant fraction of the capital stock perishes every period. Both the large scale introduction of computers in the past twenty years and the replacement of energy-intensive technologies with energy-saving ones suggest that depreciation rates may well have been higher in that period. A recent literature survey conducted by the OECD (1993) provides some evidence bearing on this point. If depreciation rates after 1970 were higher than before, then the typical capital stock series is upward biased in the second subperiod. The quality of the capital stock series is also critically contingent on the reliability of the estimate of the initial capital stock used in its calculation.

[6] The accelerator model used in this study is similar to Fair's (1984, pp. 174 -175) formulation. The so-called q-model of investment is a theoretically attractive alternative to the accelerator model.

characteristics.[7] In a simplified version of this model which is often used in macroeconometric modelling, the equilibrium capital stock is a linear function of income and the real interest rate.[8]

One of the findings of chapter 3 is that over different exchange rate regimes no stable relationship exists between the interest rate on bonds and the capital stock of a country. Therefore, the following econometric estimates will not estimate an elasticity of investment with respect to the real bond interest rate. No time series is available for the market return on capital which, in an investment equation, is the relevant variable. Hence, a procedure that directly estimates the effect of the change in the exchange rate regime will be applied. In order to deduce an equation explaining aggregate investment we start with a linear expression for the equilibrium capital stock:

$$K^*_t = \alpha Y_t + \beta \bar{r}_t \qquad (4.1)$$

The variable Y denotes real income and $\bar{r}$ stands for the market return on investment. The latter term is just modeled as a function of the exchange rate regime:

$$\bar{r}_t = \varphi_0 + \varphi_1 Regime_t \qquad (4.2)$$

Desired investment (I^*) is desired net investment (ΔK^*) plus the depreciation of the capital stock (D):

$$I^*_t = \Delta K^*_t + D_t \qquad (4.3)$$

Depreciation in any single period depends on the level of the capital stock. Since the estimates of the capital stock available are built on assumptions about

---

[7] The connection between the accelerator model and neoclassical theory is nicely explained in Dornbusch and Fischer (1984). For the Cobb-Douglas case, the desired capital stock is $K^* = (1 - v)(Y/\bar{r})$ where $(1 - v)$ is the capital share parameter, Y is output, and $\bar{r}$ denotes the return on physical investments required by the market. Alternatively, K^* can also be written as $K^* = [(1 - v)/\bar{r}]^{1/v} L$ where L is labor input. The version of the accelerator model that includes a cost of capital term is usually called the neoclassical version and was explored first by Jorgenson in a series of papers. See, e. g., Jorgenson (1971).

[8] See, e. g., Taylor (1989). Fair (1984) does not find a significant effect of the interest rate.

depreciation, these data are not suited to estimate the rate of depreciation. Hence, I follow Fair's suggestion and model the depreciation of the capital stock as a function of time.[9]

$$D_t = \phi_0 + \phi_1 t + \phi_2 t^2 \qquad (4.4)$$

Actual investment is modelled as changing over time so as to close the difference between desired and actual investment. This is a standard partial-adjustment equation:

$$\Delta I_t = \lambda(I^*_t - I_{t-1}) \qquad (4.5)$$

Inserting (4.1), (4.2), (4.3), and (4.4) into (4.5) results in the following expression:

$$\Delta I_t = \lambda\phi_0 - \lambda I_{t-1} + \lambda\phi_1 t + \lambda\phi_2 t^2 + \lambda\alpha\Delta Y_t + \lambda\beta\varphi_1 \Delta Regime_t \qquad (4.6)$$

This is the equation that will be used in the subsequent econometric work. The data used in the econometric analysis are annual data for Switzerland. The investment series is deflated aggregate investment (structures and equipment) without changes in inventories.[10] The income series is real gross domestic product. All variables are in 1980 values of Swiss francs. Given the simultaneity of investment and income, the income variable in (4.6) has to be instrumented for. The instruments used are the German real gross domestic product, the German real interest rate and lagged terms of the Swiss income and the Swiss real interest rate. Following Howe and Pigott (1992), we use as the real interest rate the long-term federal bond rate minus the average of consumer price inflation over the past three years. The variable *Regime* is just a dummy variable which is zero until 1970 and one thereafter.

Table 4.1 presents the results of two versions of the investment equation. Column A shows the basic regression. Column B adds a lagged income term as a regressor. This is a practice often followed in investment studies. It is motivated by the idea that the Y in (4.1) should be the permanent income

---

[9] Fair only uses a linear time variable in his estimates [See Fair (1984), pp. 168-169]. For the data used here, the addition of a quadratic time term leads to better results.

[10] The OECD labels this series as gross fixed capital formation.

which can be proxied by the current and lagged terms of the observed income. The reported coefficients are estimated short-run coefficients. In order to deduce the long-run coefficients they have to be divided by the coefficient of the lagged endogenous term. The coefficient of the lagged investment term indicates that it takes investment around two years to complete 50% of the adjustment to the equilibrium. The estimates of the long-run coefficient of real income are 2.623 and 2.503.[11] The inclusion of income in both estimates should effectively counter the possible argument that the capital stock in the second subperiod was only higher because of stronger economic growth, particularly in the 1980s.

The important finding reported in table 4.1 is that the measured reaction of investment to the change in exchange rate regime is positive as expected from the theory of chapter 3. The quantitative effect on the capital stock of the switch to flexible exchange rates is an increase by 13,740 million Swiss francs according to the first estimate and 8,650 million Swiss francs according to the second estimate. If we want to make an assessment of the change relative to the size of the capital stock we have to make use of an estimate of this series. The estimated equations do not allow to compute a series of the equilibrium capital stock K^* because the parameter φ_0 is not estimated and the parameter β is not identified. Hence, we rely on the estimate of the K-series calculated by Büttler, Ettlin, and Ruoss (1987). If the above numbers are set into relation with the level of the capital stock in 1971 - the year of the regime switch - we find that the two numbers correspond to changes of 2.7% and 1.7%, respectively.

---

[11] It is obvious from the investment equation that investment is strongly affected by income. A first cause of income variations are changes in the labor input in the production process (see also footnote 7 on page 76). Naturally, it would be interesting to find out whether exchange rate uncertainty actually influenced the amount of time people were willing to work. The problem with the historical data is that the variations in the work hours in the period around the regime shift are dominated by the decrease of work hours during the recession of 1975 and 1976. There is no evidence that the increased exchange rate uncertainty was the cause of the observed reduction in work hours.

Table 4.1 Estimates of Investment Equations*

Equation	A	B
Constant	732.118	749.849
	(0.708)	(0.790)
I_{t-1}	-0.223	-0.266
	(3.877)	(4.824)
t	158.496	202.003
	(1.312)	(1.803)
t^2	1.945	1.947
	(1.104)	(1.203)
ΔY_t^{ins}	0.585	0.475
	(6.363)	(5.088)
ΔY_{t-1}		0.191
		(2.739)
$\Delta Regime_t$	3063.959	2300.964
	(2.209)	(1.765)
$\bar{R}^2$	0.551	0.622
DW	1.470	1.789
SEE	1337.533	1228.227

* Numbers in parentheses are absolute values of the t-statistic.

4.3 Conclusions

The conclusion to be drawn from this empirical exercise is that the transition to flexible exchange rates in the early 1970s led to an increase in the Swiss capital stock. The econometric estimates point towards a rather modest increase of about 2%. Qualitatively, this finding fits well with the theoretical conjecture arrived at in chapter 3: The implication of the equilibrium analysis proposed there simply states that the direction of capital flows initiated by the regime switch can be inferred from the sign of the emerging foreign exchange risk premium. Under flexible exchange rates investments in the country with a positive foreign exchange risk premium become more attractive to domestic and foreign investors. Hence, an increase in the Swiss physical capital stock had to be expected.

What remains to be explored is the effect on income of the transition to flexible exchange rates. There are both distributional and aggregate effects. The documented increase in the capital stock very likely led to an increase in wages and land rent and reduced the return on capital. Thus, the regime switch favored labor and land owners and harmed owners of capital in Switzerland. Secondly, we have noted that the return on capital in Switzerland had been lower than in the U. S. and many other countries before the transition and that this differential increased after the transition. As was shown in section 3.6 a regime change that increases the difference in capital returns between countries tends to reduce the sum of expected incomes of these countries. From the viewpoint of efficient capital allocation it is thus doubtful that a flexible exchange rate for the Swiss franc is advantageous to Switzerland and the world. It seems that - with accompanying transfer payments - everybody could be made better off if some of the savings allocated to investment in Switzerland were to flow out. A fixed exchange rate is likely to produce just that situation. It has to be kept in mind, though, that the quantitative effect of the regime switch found in this study is rather modest. Moreover, the group of countries committed to exchange rate stabilization under the system of Bretton Woods was larger than the European Monetary Union which, at present, is the only system Switzerland considers joining. This means that the advantage to the members of the European Monetary Union of an entry by Switzerland is probably not very large, at least not with respect to attracting capital at present allocated to Switzerland.

Appendix 4: Data and Sources

I_t: real investment (gross fixed capital formation, source: Swiss National Bank)
Y_t: real gross domestic product (source: Swiss National Bank)
ΔY_t^{ins}: instrumented change in real gross domestic product (the instruments used are the German real gross domestic product, the German real interest rate and lagged terms of the Swiss income and the Swiss real interest rate)

Time	I_t	Y_t	ΔY_t^{ins}
1950	9525	60465	4739.206
1951	11550	65025	5385.212
1952	11720	65535	1605.527
1953	12785	67725	156.995
1954	14245	71450	2150.418
1955	15500	76060	5645.091
1956	17360	80905	3986.477
1957	18190	84135	4732.312
1958	16480	82335	1515.195
1959	19170	87485	2259.923
1960	21765	93445	5476.679
1961	25145	101250	4518.148
1962	27600	106335	4443.580
1963	29640	111605	4024.404
1964	32215	117295	6214.985
1965	31400	120890	5548.853
1966	31135	123805	3090.646
1967	31135	127520	486.450
1968	32110	132235	5174.685
1969	34050	139650	8109.926
1970	36955	148530	7127.346

Time	I_t	Y_t	ΔY_t^{ins}
1971	40655	154880	4655.199
1972	42765	160235	5624.999
1973	44130	165300	7314.507
1974	42115	167245	2861.366
1975	36540	156020	-3275.262
1976	32795	154710	31.394
1977	33255	158360	622.390
1978	35105	159300	2671.421
1979	36880	163180	4460.389
1980	40500	170330	3768.162
1981	41590	172780	2159.799
1982	40525	171180	-727.000
1983	42190	172900	960.505
1984	43935	175960	4034.381
1985	46260	182485	2183.082
1986	49910	187715	3906.687
1987	53620	191525	3324.933
1988	57340	197080	6079.014
1989	60650	204690	6615.458
1990	61990	209190	9041.516

5

The Effects of Variable Inflation on the Capital Stock and Consumption

It is a wide-spread notion that monetary policy affects output via inflation risk. Chapter 2 explored a major channel through which inflation risk works. The theoretical analysis of chapter 3 also focused on the spread of unpredictable variations, namely, variations in the real exchange rate. It seems appropriate to conclude this book with an analysis of the effects of a change in the dispersion of predictable variations. This chapter, therefore, deals with the spread of predictable variations of inflation induced by monetary policy. It draws attention to the fact that this variability, too, can matter for capital accumulation and consumption.

Contrary to the effect of inflation uncertainty, the effect of predictable variations is not a well researched area.[1] Friedman (1977) saw the central problem of inflation variability in the complication it adds to the task of extracting signals about relative prices from observed absolute prices. With this argument he established the precept that what matters about inflation variations is the induced uncertainty. This outlook is apparent in the work that considers the effect of inflation variability on growth via savings and portfolio decisions. In Gertler's and Grinols' (1982) model unpredictable inflation variations (caused by monetary policy) induce individuals to hold more money and less real capital. Accordingly, a decrease in inflation uncertainty increases the capital stock and leads to a step increase in output. Sweeney (1987) develops a rational expectations macro-model with an asset demand system based on a capital asset pricing structure. Again, the focus is on unpredictable

---

[1] See, for example, the papers presented at a conference on *inflation uncertainty* sponsored by the Federal Reserve Bank of Cleveland and published as a special issue (1993) of the Journal of Money, Credit, and Banking.

84 *Monetary Regimes, Risk, and International Capital Accumulation*

inflation variations. Sweeney concludes that a decrease in inflation uncertainty can either increase or reduce the capital stock.

In the econometric work the focus on the aspect of unpredictability of inflation has led researchers to devise ever more sophisticated methods to construct proxies for inflation risk. Lately, so-called ARCH processes have been used that permit proper estimation of the time varying variance of the inflation forecast. Interestingly, Jansen (1989) has found no effect of such a measure of inflation risk on U. S. output. His findings lead me to the following considerations. First, U. S. output may historically have been unaffected by inflationary uncertainty (a middle position between Gertler-Grinols' and Sweeney's propositions). Second, while inflation risk does not seem to matter, predictable inflation variations might still do so. The following sections formally address this second point. A monetary growth model devised by Dornbusch and Frenkel (1973) serves as the basis for the following analysis.[2]

5.1 Steady Inflation

The Dornbusch-Frenkel model of inflation and growth assumes that real money balances provide "shopping services". This means that money is valued because holding it reduces the amount of output that in its absence would be devoted to sustaining the exchange system. Hence, money is treated as a factor of production. In the following, I summarize the Dornbusch-Frenkel model. Output per capita net of capital maintenance is $g(k, n) \equiv f(k) - nk$ where k is the capital-labor ratio and n is the exogenously given growth rate of the labor force.[3] Money enters the economy via transfer payments that are totally unrelated to the individual's holdings of real money balances.[4]

Dornbusch and Frenkel chose a particularly simple formulation of the services of money: output available for consumption, called y here, is a

---

[2] Monetary growth models were initially developed to assess the effect of the level of inflation on capital accumulation.

[3] As long as $f' \geq n$, the economy operates efficiently in that an increase in the per capita capital stock leads to a non-negative change in per capita output.

[4] This assumption makes sure that money is not an interest-bearing asset.

fraction $1 - v(m)$ of output $g(k, n)$ where this fraction is an increasing function of real money balances denoted by m.[5]

$$y = g(k, n)[1 - v(m)], \text{ with } g' > 0, g'' < 0, 0 \leq v \leq 1, v' < 0, v'' \geq 0 \quad (5.1)$$

The price level and hence the level of real balances are endogenous variables. As will become clear the key policy variable is the growth rate rather than the level of nominal balances supplied to the private sector. The growth rate of the nominal money supply determines inflation (i. e., the cost of holding money) thereby determining the equilibrium level of real balances.

Figure 5.1 shows two selected forms of the $[1 - v(m)]$-fraction that fulfill the conditions of (5.1). The one labeled (a) is based on a quadratic $v(m)$-function while the one labeled (b) is derived from the function $v(m) = m^{-\alpha}$ where $\alpha > 0$ and $m > 1$. The symbol m^* denotes the satiation level of real balances. Satiation is reached when additional balances do not increase the productivity of money any further.[6] In the quadratic case there is satiation at a finite level of m while in the second case satiation is reached only at an infinite level of m.

The $[1 - v(m)]$-function depends, inter alia, on the payment technology available in a country. Technological advances in the payment system like the introduction of credit cards or electronic banking make a given stock of real balances more productive and imply an upward shift in the depicted curve. Alternatively, political crises that hamper the use of money or make cash transactions necessary where previously credit transactions were the rule imply a downward shift in the curve. Thus, the present framework nicely captures some basic notions regarding the role of money in the economy.

---

[5] See their footnote 15 for an alternative specification. In their notation the variable called y here is called c. We reserve the symbol c for later use.

[6] The upper limit of the $[1 - v(m)]$-fraction is not necessarily 1. There may be a non-zero fraction of output lost to transactions which is not reducible by additional money.

86 *Monetary Regimes, Risk, and International Capital Accumulation*

(a) $1 - v(m) = 1 - (\zeta + \eta m + \omega m^2)$ with $m \leq -\dfrac{\eta}{2\omega}$, $1 > \zeta > 0$, $\eta < 0$, $\omega > 0$

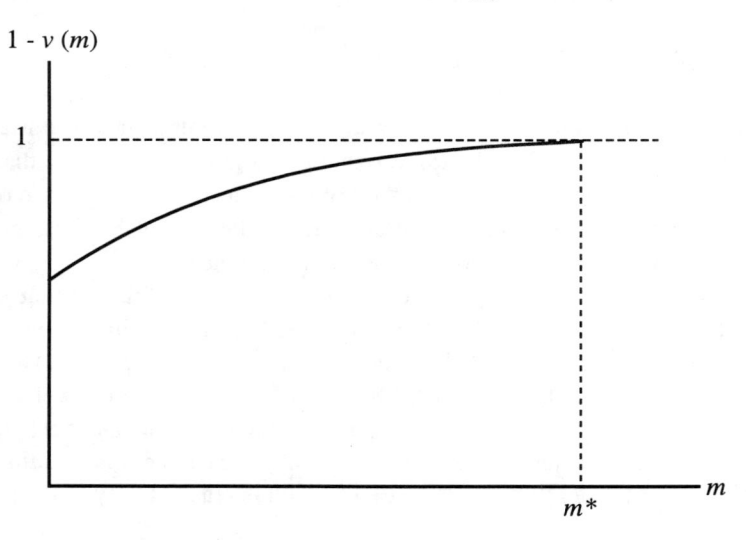

$1 - v(m)$

m^*

m

(b) $1 - v(m) = 1 - m^{-\alpha}$ with $m > 1$, $\alpha > 1$

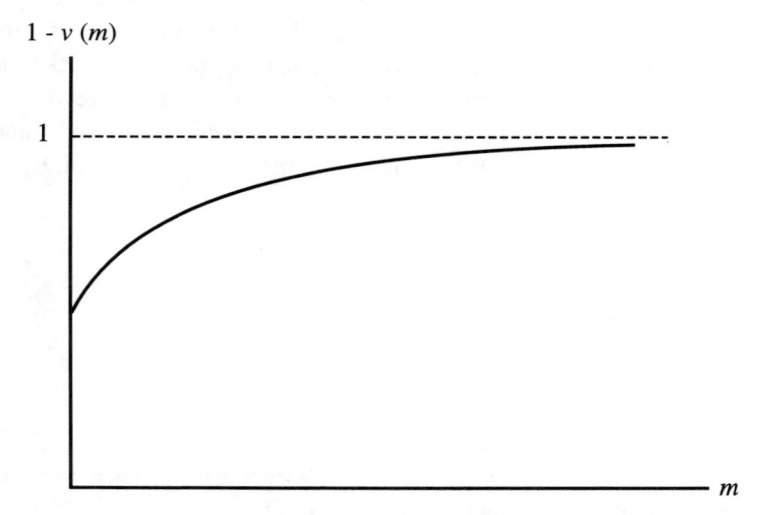

$1 - v(m)$

m

Figure 5.1 *Two Possible Specifications of the Productivity of Money, i. e., of the Fraction* $[1 - v(m)]$

The representative individual maximizes a utility function that depends only on consumption. Since an explicit hypothesis about the services of money is introduced, money has no separate role in the utility function.[7] Let ρ be the rate of time preference. The individual then maximizes his discounted stream of utility

$$\int_0^\infty u(y) \, e^{-\rho t} \, dt \tag{5.2}$$

subject to the budget constraint

$$y = g(k, n)[1 - v(m)] + h - (\pi + n)m - \dot{k} - \dot{m} \; . \tag{5.3}$$

Here, h denotes transfer payments, π is the inflation rate, and dotted variables are changes of the respective variables over time. In the steady state, k and m are constant and hence $\dot{k}$ and $\dot{m}$ are zero. Since $\dot{m} = m(\mu - n - \pi)$, where μ is the rate of monetary growth, we know that in the steady state inflation equals the excess of money growth over population growth (i. e., $\pi = \mu - n$). Moreover, since $h = \mu m$, (5.3) reduces to (5.1) when the system is in the steady state. For convenience we write the functions g and v and their derivatives g' and v' without their respective arguments k and m. The steady state optimality condition for the capital stock is

$$g'(1 - v) = \rho \; . \tag{5.4}$$

The counterpart condition for real balances is[8]

$$-v'g = \rho + \pi + n \; . \tag{5.5}$$

---

[7] Sidrauski (1967) is the standard reference for growth models with money in the utility function. See also Stein's (1971) survey of monetary growth models.

[8] The Euler equations $\dfrac{\partial H}{\partial k} = \dfrac{\partial}{\partial t}\left(\dfrac{\partial H}{\partial \dot{k}}\right)$ and $\dfrac{\partial H}{\partial m} = \dfrac{\partial}{\partial t}\left(\dfrac{\partial H}{\partial \dot{m}}\right)$ lead to the stated conditions for steady state optimality (i. e., for $\dot{y} = 0$). H is $u(y) \, e^{-\rho t}$ after substituting y with the expression from the budget constraint [equation (5.3)] in the utility function.

Under the assumption that $y(k, m)$ is a strictly concave function [formally expressed as $(\partial^2 y/\partial k^2)(\partial^2 y/\partial m^2) > (\partial^2 y/\partial k \partial m)^2$] an increase in money growth and hence in inflation unambiguously reduces real balances, the capital stock, and consumption. Hence, the Dornbusch-Frenkel model leads to the same qualitative result regarding the effect of inflation on capital accumulation as the model of Feldstein, Green and Sheshinski (1978) which is the opposite of Tobin's (1965) result.[9]

5.2 Variable Inflation

Instead of a constant money growth rate as before, households now face a variable money growth rate. Money growth switches between a high money growth rate, μ_B, and a low money growth rate, μ_A.[10] It is assumed that the average money growth is $(\mu_A + \mu_B)/2$. These changes in money growth are predictable reactions by the central bank to regularly occurring events in the economy. Ultimately, we want to know how the amplitude of these predictable changes affects the capital stock. Henceforth, the term variability is used to mean the spread of these predictable variations.

Whenever the growth rate of the money supply changes, a step change in real money balances results. If the monetary authority were just to switch from μ_B to μ_A, or vice versa, the step change in desired real balances would induce a jump in the price level. This is the necessary outcome in a model with nominal price flexibility. In reality, there is little evidence of such discontinuous changes of the price level. Hence, we introduce a technical condition that rules these changes out: we assume that the monetary authority follows what Auernheimer (1974) called the honest government's guide to inflationary taxation. Under this rule the monetary authority makes step adjustments in the money supply whenever it changes the growth rate of money. When money growth is reduced, for example, then the money supply is increased just enough so that no step adjustment of the price level is necessary. This practice is called honest because it prevents once-and-for-all

---

[9] See Wang and Yip (1992) for a recent survey of results obtained from different models based on individual optimization.

[10] Money growth can be positive or negative. However, we want to restrict μ_A to be larger than $-\rho$. This prevents m from reaching the satiation level m^*.

capital levies on money holdings.[11] It follows from the policy rule described above that inflation, except in instants where money growth changes, is $\pi = \mu - n$ (i. e., $\pi_A = \mu_A - n$ and $\pi_B = \mu_B - n$).[12] As a result, real money balances alternate between m_A and m_B depending on whether inflation runs at π_A or at π_B.

The second change introduced into the basic Dornbusch-Frenkel setup is the addition of an international dimension. We assume that installed physical capital cannot be moved from one country to another. This can be justified with adjustment costs of investment that are too high compared to the possible gains of internationally relocating physical capital. As a result, households have to choose a capital stock to which they adhere (in contrast to real balances) no matter what the inflation rate is.[13]

Even with a constant capital stock, output varies with changes in the inflation rate: it rises when inflation falls and declines when inflation rises. This is because the level of real balances affects output available for consumption. These changes, however, have no effect on consumption since we postulate a frictionless international capital market with a fixed world interest rate. The individuals will keep their consumption at the average level because they have declining marginal utility of income. The possibility of running a current account deficit (i. e., to borrow) or a surplus (i. e., to lend) works as an insurance against output fluctuations and allows households to smooth consumption perfectly.[14] Thus, variability of output as such has no effect on households' utility. What has an effect is the influence of inflationary

---

[11] When the governments follows this rule it does not maximize its income from money creation. In order to sidestep issues of dynamic consistency we have to assume that the monetary authority has credibly committed itself to this policy.

[12] The variance of π (as well as of μ) is $\left[(\pi_B - \pi_A)/2\right]^2 = \left[(\mu_B - \mu_A)/2\right]^2$. Hence, the standard deviation is just $(\pi_B - \pi_A)/2 = (\mu_B - \mu_A)/2$, which is the width of the π (and of the μ)-band.

[13] Between changes in the inflation rate investments or disinvestments would tend to adjust the capital stock to the level that is optimal under any given inflation rate. We can discard these deviations from the average level of the capital stock by assuming that the investments and disinvestments involved are small relative to the capital stock and that inflation changes occur frequently.

[14] The model predicts that realizations of high inflation rates worsen the current account while low rates of inflation improve the current account. As in most international models with intertemporal optimization, we assume that ρ is equal to the world real interest rate. We rule out any permanent indebtedness.

90 Monetary Regimes, Risk, and International Capital Accumulation

variability on the average level of output. Here, we introduce the notation c for consumption [$c = (y_A + y_B)/2$] where y_A and y_B are the two levels of net output associated with the two levels of inflation. The introduced changes lead to the replacement of y by c in the utility function. The resulting new first order conditions are:[15]

$$g'(1 - 0.5v_A - 0.5v_B) = \rho \tag{5.6}$$

$$- v'_A g = \rho + \pi_A + n = \rho + \mu_A \tag{5.7}$$

$$- v'_B g = \rho + \pi_B + n = \rho + \mu_B \tag{5.8}$$

Here v_A and v_B stand for $v(m_A)$ and $v(m_B)$, while v'_A and v'_B stand for $v'(m_A)$ and $v'(m_B)$. Although (5.6), (5.7), and (5.8) cannot be solved for k, m_A, m_B, and c for standard functional forms of g and v, we can establish comparative static results following Samuelson (1947).

The experiment we conduct is a reduction in the difference between μ_B and μ_A while holding average money growth unchanged (i. e., $d\mu_A = - d\mu_B > 0$).[16] Figure 5.2 shows the two alternative price level paths. The reduction in money growth variability means a move from a price level path as exemplified by the dotted line to the solid line. The solid line is the one with the smaller inflation variance. The thin solid line depicts the price level path with the average inflation common to the two other paths but with zero inflation variability.

---

[15] The new optimality conditions come from Euler equations for m_A, m_B and k where the y in the utility function is replaced by

$$0.5[g(1 - v_A) + h_A - (\pi_A + n)m_A - \dot{k} - \dot{m}_A]$$
$$+ 0.5[g(1 - v_B) + h_B - (\pi_B + n)m_B - \dot{k} - \dot{m}_B] \, .$$

[16] In this context, the Lucas critique naturally springs to mind [See Lucas (1976)]. The model set out in this chapter describes rational forward looking individuals. Hence, it is natural to assume that individuals know about the possibility of a change in policy. This means that they will evaluate the consequences of a possible increase or decrease in monetary variability (i. e., a deviation from the initial levels of μ_B and μ_A to some wider or narrower money growth band). In the present model this just imposes the condition that the various possible money growth bands must be grouped around μ_B and μ_A in such a manner that the average income level (the argument in the utility function) remains unaffected.

ln (P)

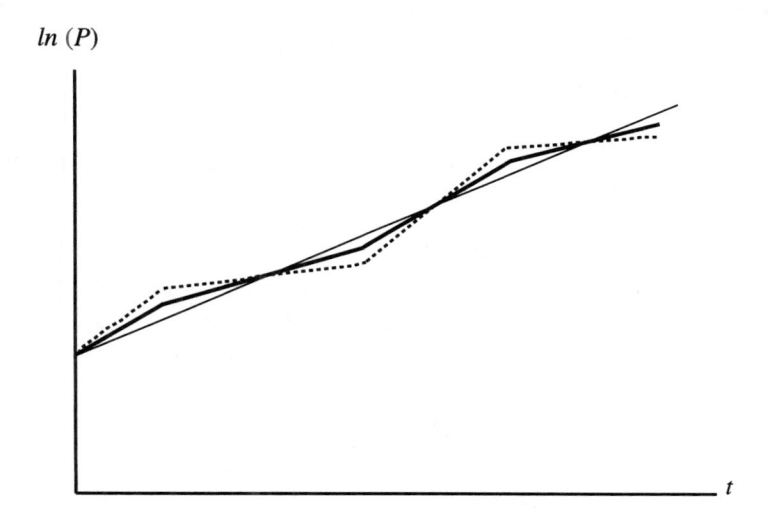

Figure 5.2 *Price Level Paths with Equal Average Inflation but Different Inflation Variance*

The effects of the reduction in monetary and hence inflationary variability (the standard deviation of μ and π both decrease by $d\mu_A$) can be found by totally differentiating the system of equations (5.6), (5.7), and (5.8). The determinant of the new system, Δ, can be written as

$$\Delta = 0.5g\{v_A'' [(1 - v_A)gg''v_B'' + (g'v_B')^2] + v_B'' [(1 - v_B)gg''v_A'' + (g'v_A')^2]\} < 0 .$$

The determinant is negative by virtue of the previously used assumption of concavity of the $y(k, m)$ function. The comparative static change of m_A (the level of real balances with the lower rate of inflation) due to the narrowing of the monetary growth band is $dm_A/d\mu_A$. This ratio, interpreted as the comparative static derivative $(\partial m_A/\partial \mu_A)$, is

$$\frac{\partial m_A}{\partial \mu_A} = - \frac{0.5}{\Delta}\{[(1 - v_A)gg''v_B'' + (g')^2 v_A' v_B'] + [(1 - v_B)gg''v_A'' + (g'v_A')^2]\} < 0 .$$

This expression is unambiguously negative because of the condition used before and since $(1 - v_A) > (1 - v_B)$ and $|v_B'| > |v_A'|$ according to (5.1). The corresponding expression for the change in m_B is

$$\frac{\partial m_B}{\partial \mu_A} = \frac{0.5}{\Delta} \{[(1 - v_B)gg''v_A'' + (g')^2 v_A' v_B'] + [(1 - v_A)gg''v_A'' + (g'v_A')^2]\} \gtreqless 0.$$

Unlike $\partial m_A/\partial \mu_A$ the sign of $\partial m_B/\partial \mu_A$ is not definite because $(1 - v_A) > (1 - v_B)$ and $|v_B'| > |v_A'|$ now work towards a positive sign of the first term in brackets. The key results, however, concern the reaction of the capital stock and consumption to the reduction in the standard deviation of money growth:

$$\frac{\partial k}{\partial \mu_A} = -\frac{0.5\ gg'}{\Delta} (v_A' v_B'' - v_B' v_A'') \gtreqless 0$$

$$\frac{\partial c}{\partial \mu_A} = -\frac{1}{\Delta} c[(g')^2 - g''] (v_A' v_B'' - v_B' v_A'') \gtreqless 0$$

In both expressions the parts before $(v_A' v_B'' - v_B' v_A'')$ are positive. As a result, the signs of $\partial k/\partial \mu_A$ and $\partial c/\partial \mu_A$ are always equal and hinge on the sign of $(v_A' v_B'' - v_B' v_A'')$, that is, on the curvature of the $v(m)$-function. We can say more about the conditions under which $(v_A' v_B'' - v_B' v_A'')$ is of either sign. It is straightforward that $v_A'' = v_B''$ is a sufficient (not a necessary) condition for a positive sign since $|v_B'| > |v_A'|$. We call the case with the positive sign (reducing the variance of inflation raises both capital stock and consumption) the standard result. Hence, when the variations in real balances induced by the monetary variability occur in a region of the $v(m)$-curve where v''' is zero then capital stock and consumption rise with a reduction in monetary variability.

If $v(m)$ is a quadratic function the outlined condition is met. The quadratic $v(m)$-function, introduced in section 5.1, is one for which satiation with real balances is reached at a finite level of m. This functional form produces the standard result. As a counter-example consider the case $v(m) = m^{-\alpha}$, also introduced before. Obviously, $1 - m^{-\alpha}$ goes to one only when m goes to infinity. This specification of the $v(m)$-function satisfies

$0 \leq v \leq 1$, $v' < 0$, $v'' \geq 0$ (for $m > 1$) and its form is enough to make $\partial k/\partial \mu_A$ and $\partial c/\partial \mu_A$ always negative.[17]

As a last functional form consider the case where $v(m) = e^{-\beta m}$. This specification also satisfies the conditions imposed on (5.1). In this case, $v'_A/v''_A = v'_B/v''_B = -1/\beta$ and therefore $v'_A v''_B - v'_B v''_A = 0$. I call this the *steadiness equivalent* case. Corresponding to the concept of certainty equivalence, this is the case where - independent of the level of inflationary variability - the outcome for the capital stock and consumption is always the same as with steady inflation.

Further-reaching conclusions are necessarily tentative. It can be argued, for example, that it seems unrealistic to assume a curvature of $v(m)$ that would lead to an infinite money stock as the inflation (or rather deflation) reaches a level where the marginal cost of holding money becomes zero. This suggests a functional form of $v(m)$ like the quadratic case discussed before. It is possible, however, that $v(m)$ has the curvature of $m^{-\alpha}$ or $e^{-\beta m}$ over some range - maybe for rather high rates of inflation and low values of real balances - while over the range of low rates of inflation - close to the satiation level - $v(m)$ resembles more the quadratic case.[18] If this is the case and central banks are concerned with attainable levels of consumption, they should make sure they keep both the level of inflation and the variance of inflation low. Under the same premise, countries with low rates of inflation should be more oriented towards reducing monetary variability than countries with high rates of inflation.

5.3   Conclusions

The present model shows how fully predictable monetary variability can influence capital accumulation and consumption in a small open economy. With a view to econometric work we conclude from the present study that it is wrong to assume a priori that predictable inflation variations are without effects. Except in the described case of steadiness equivalence described above variability does indeed matter.

---

[17] This results because $v'_A v''_B - v'_B v''_A = -\alpha^2(\alpha + 1)(m_A m_B)^{-\alpha-1}(m_B^{-1} - m_A^{-1}) < 0$.

[18] One can also imagine cases where a reduction in inflationary variability increase output over some range of the variance while further steadying of inflation has the opposite effect.

The effect of inflation variability that emerges is basically due to the fact that the marginal product of money decreases as the money stock rises. Despite this non-linearity there exists a case where inflation variability is neutral with respect to investment and consumption. In general, variability of inflation can increase or decrease capital stock and consumption. The direction of the effect of inflation variability depends on the specifics of the productive services of money in the range over which real balances vary due to inflation variability. Hence, the effect can be positive or negative depending on the average level of inflation. Therefore, even countries with identical production possibilities and identical monetary systems can experience qualitatively different effects of inflation variability if their average inflation rates differ. Similarly, a country can experience that reducing inflation variability at a certain level of mean inflation pays off in terms of consumption while at another level of inflation further smoothing is without gain or even costly.

References

Aizenman, Joshua, 1992, Exchange Rate Flexibility, Volatility, and Domestic and Foreign Direct Investment. IMF Staff Papers, 39, 890-922.

Ammer, John, 1994, Inflation, Inflation Risk, and Stock Returns. International Finance Discussion Papers No. 464, Board of Governors of the Federal Reserve System.

Argy, Victor, 1994, International Macroeconomics. Routledge, London.

Arrow, Kenneth, J., 1971, Essays in the Theory of Risk-Bearing. North-Holland, Amsterdam.

Auernheimer, Leonardo, 1974, The Honest Government's Guide to the Revenue from the Creation of Money. Journal of Political Economy, 82, 598-606.

Backus, David K., Patrick J. Kehoe, and Finn E. Kydland, 1993, International Business Cycles: Theory and Evidence, NBER Working Paper No. 4493.

Barro, Robert J., 1974, Are Government Bonds Net Wealth? Journal of Political Economy, 82, 1095-1117.

Bernanke, Ben, Henning Bohn, and Peter C. Reiss, 1988, Alternative Non-Nested Specification Tests of Time-Series Investment Models. Journal of Econometrics, 37, 293-326.

Blanchard, Olivier J., and Stanley Fischer, 1989, Lectures in Macroeconomics. The MIT Press, Cambridge, MA.

Branson, William H., and Dale W. Henderson, 1985, The Specification and Influence of Asset Markets. In Ronald W. Jones, and Peter B. Kenen (eds.) Handbook of International Economics, Vol 2, Chapter 15. North-Holland, Amsterdam.

Büttler, Hans-Jürg, Franz Ettlin and Eveline Ruoss, 1987, Empirische Schätzung des Wachstums der potentiellen Produktion in der Schweiz. Geld, Währung und Konjunktur: Quartalsheft der Schweizerischen Nationalbank, 1, 61-71.

Clark, Peter C., 1979, Investment in the 1970s: Theory, Performance, and Prediction. Brookings Papers on Economic Activity, 1, 73-113.

Clower, Robert W., 1967, A Reconsideration of the Microfoundations of Monetary Theory. Western Economic Journal, 6, 1-8.

Debreu, Gerard, 1959, The Theory of Value. Wiley, New York.

Dooley, Michael P., Jeffrey A. Frankel, and Donald J. Mathieson, 1987, International Capital Mobility: What do Savings-Investment Correlations Tell Us? IMF Staff Papers, 34, 503-530.

Dornbusch, Rudiger, 1983, Exchange Rate Risk and the Macroeconomics of Exchange Rate Determination. In R. Hawkins, et. al. (eds.) Research in International Business and Finance, Vol. 3, JAI Press, Greenwich.

Dornbusch, Rudiger, and Stanley Fischer, 1984, Macroeconomics. 3rd edition, MacGraw-Hill, New York.

Dornbusch, Rudiger, and Jacob A. Frenkel, 1973, Inflation and Growth: Alternative Approaches. Journal of Money, Credit, and Banking, 50, 141-156.

Drèze, Jaques H., and Franco Modigliani, 1972, Consumption Decision under Uncertainty. Journal of Economic Theory, 5, 308-335.

Driffill John, Grayham E. Mizon, and Alistair Ulph, 1990, Costs of Inflation. In Benjamin M. Friedman and Frank H. Hahn (eds.) Handbook of Monetary Economics, Vol. 2, Chapter 19. North-Holland, Amsterdam.

Eichengreen, Barry, 1988, Real Exchange Rate Behavior under Alternative International Monetary Regimes: Interwar Evidence. European Economic Review, 32, 363-371.

Fair, Ray C., 1984, Specification, Estimation, and Analysis of Macroeconometric Models. Harvard University Press, Cambridge, MA.

Fama, Eugene F., 1981, Stock Returns, Real Activity, Inflation, and Money. American Economic Review, 71, 545-565.

Fama, Eugene F. and William Schwert, 1977, Asset Returns and Inflation. Journal of Financial Economics, 5, 115-146.

Feldstein, Martin S., Jerry Green, and Eytan Sheshinski, 1978, Inflation and Taxes in a Growing Economy with Debt and Equity Finance. Journal of Political Economy, 86, 53-70.

Feldstein, Martin S., and Charles Horioka, 1980, Domestic Saving and International Capital Flows. The Economic Journal, 90, 314-329.

Fleming, J. Marcus, 1962, Domestic Financial Policies under Fixed and under Floating Exchange Rates. IMF Staff Papers, 9, 369-379.

Frankel, Jeffrey A., 1979, The Diversifiability of Exchange Risk. Journal of International Economics, 9, 379-393.

Frankel, Jeffrey A., 1986, The Implications of Mean-Variance Optimization for Four Questions in International Macroeconomics. Journal of International Money and Finance, 5, S53-S75.

Frankel, Jeffrey A., 1991, Quantifying International Capital Mobility in the 1980s. In B. D. Bernheim and J. B. Shoven (eds.) National Saving and Economic Performance. The University of Chicago Press, Chicago, IL.

Frankel, Jeffrey A., and Alan T. MacArthur, 1988, Political vs. Currency Premia in International Real Interest Rate Differentials. European Economic Review, 32, 1083-1121.

Friedman, Milton, 1977, Nobel Lecture: Inflation and Unemployment. Journal of Political Economy, 85, 451-472.

Gertler, Mark, and Earl L. Grinols, 1982, Monetary Randomness and Investment. Journal of Monetary Economics, 10, 239-258.

Grandmont, Jean-Michel, and Yves Younes, 1973, On the Efficiency of a Monetary Equilibrium. Review of Economic Studies, 40, 149-165.

Grinols, Earl L., and Stephen J. Turnovsky, 1991, Stochastic Equilibrium and Exchange Rate Determination in a Small Open Economy with Risk Averse Optimizing Agents. NBER Working Paper No. 3651.

Hall, Robert E., 1988, Intertemporal Substitution in Consumption. Journal of Political Economy, 96, 339-357.

Helpman, Elhanan, 1981, An Exploration of the Theory of Exchange-Rate Regimes. Journal of Political Economy, 89, 865-890.

Helpman, Elhanan, and Assaf Razin, 1982, A Comparison of Exchange Rate Regimes in the Presence of Imperfect Capital Markets. International Economic Review, 23, 365-388.

Hey, John D., 1979, Uncertainty in Microeconomics. New York University Press, New York.

Hirshleifer, Jack, 1965, Investment Decisions under Uncertainty: Choice Theoretic Approaches. Quarterly Journal of Economics, 74, 509-536.

Howe, Howard, and Charles Pigott, 1992, Determinants of Long-Term Interest Rates: An Empirical Study of Several Industrial Countries. Federal Reserve Bank of New York, Quarterly Review, 16, 12-28.

Inflation Uncertainty, 1993, A Conference Sponsored by the Federal Reserve Bank of Cleveland. Journal of Money, Credit, and Banking, 25, Part 2.

Jansen, Dale W., 1989, Does Inflation Uncertainty Affect Output Growth? Further Evidence. Federal Reserve Bank of St. Louis, Review, 71, 43-54.

Jorgenson, Dale W., 1971, Econometric Studies on Investment Behavior: A Survey. Journal of Economic Literature, 9, 1111-1147.

Kupiec, Paul, 1991, Stock Market Volatility in OECD Countries: Recent Trends, Consequences for the Real Economy, and Proposals for Reform. OECD Economic Studies, 17, 31-62.

Lucas, Robert E., 1976, Econometric Policy Evaluation: A Critique. Carnegie-Rochester Conference Series on Public Policy, 1, 19-46.

Lucas, Robert E., 1982, Interest Rates and Currency Prices in a Two-Country World. Journal of Monetary Economics, 10, 335-359.

MacDougall, G. Donald A., 1960, The Benefits and Costs of Private Investment from Abroad: A Theoretical Approach. Economic Record, 36, 13-35.

Mirman, Leonard J., 1971, Uncertainty and Optimal Consumption Decisions. Econometrica, 39, 179-185.

Mundell, Robert A., 1960, The Monetary Dynamics of International Adjustment under Fixed and Flexible Exchange Rates. Quarterly Journal of Economics, 74, 227-257.

Mundell, Robert A., 1961, A Theory of Optimum Currency Areas. American Economic Review, 51, 657-665.

Mussa, Michael L., 1986, Nominal Exchange Rate Regimes and the Behavior of Real Exchange Rates: Evidence and Implications. Carnegie-Rochester Conference Series on Public Policy, 25, 117-214.

Niehans, Jürg, 1975, Some Doubts about the Efficacy of Monetary Policy under Flexible Exchange Rates. Journal of International Economics, 5, 275-281.

Niehans, Jürg, 1984, International Monetary Economics. The Johns Hopkins University Press. Baltimore.

OECD, 1993, Methods Used by OECD Countries to Measure Stocks of Fixed Capital. National Accounts: Sources and Methods. No. 2, Statistics Directorate, Paris.

Patinkin, Don, 1964, Money, Interest, and Prices. 2d ed., Harper & Row, New York.

Poole, William, 1970, Optimal Choice of Monetary Policy Instruments in a Simple Stochastic Macromodel. Quarterly Journal of Economics, 84, 197-216.

Pratt, John W., 1964, Risk Aversion in the Small and in the Large. Econometrica, 32, 122-136.

Samuelson, Paul A., 1947, Foundations of Economic Analysis. Harvard University Press, Cambridge, MA.

Sandmo, Agnar, 1970, The Effect of Uncertainty on Saving Decisions. Review of Economic Studies, 37, 353-360.

Seldon, Larry, 1979, An OCE Analysis of the Effect of Uncertainty on Saving under Risk Preference Independence. Review of Economic Studies, 46, 73-82.

Sidrauski, Miguel, 1967, Rational Choice and Patterns of Growth in a Monetary Economy. American Economic Review, 57, 534-544.

Stein, Jerome L., 1971, Money and Capacity Growth. Columbia University Press, New York.

Stockman, Alan C., 1980, A Theory of Exchange Rate Determination. Journal of Political Economy, 88, 673-698.

Svensson, Lars E. O., 1987, Trade in Nominal Assets: Monetary Policy, and Price Level and Exchange Rate Risk. NBER Working Paper No. 2417.

Svensson, Lars E. O., 1989, Trade in Nominal Assets: Monetary Policy, and Price Level and Exchange Rate Risk. Journal of International Economics, 26, 1-28.

Sweeney, Richard J., 1987, Some Macro Implications of Risk. Journal of Money, Credit, and Banking, 19, 222-234.

Taylor, John B., 1989, Monetary Policy and the Stability of Macroeconomic Relationships. Journal of Applied Econometrics, 4, 161-178.

Tesar, Linda L., 1991, Savings, Investment and International Capital Flows. Journal of International Economics, 31, 55-78.

Tobin, James, 1965, Money and Economic Growth. Econometrica, 33, 671- 684.

Wang, Ping, and Chong K. Yip, 1992, Alternative Approaches to Money and Growth. Journal of Money, Credit, and Banking, 24, 553-562.

Index

activist policy, 23
after-tax return, 1, 9
aggregation, 46, 46n
Aizenman, 7n, 33, 40
Ammer, 9
ARCH processes, 84
Argi, 6n
Arrow, 8, 8n
asymmetric wealth accumulation, 58
Auernheimer, 88

Backus, 8
Barro, 49n
Bernanke, 75
Blanchard, 29n
Bohn, 75
bond
 credits, 60n
 debts, 60n, 71
 demand, 46, 47n
 generic type of, 45
 supply, 46, 49n
bonds as obligations of the private sector, 49
Branson, 42n
Bretton Woods system, 5, 80
Büttler, 78

capital
 asset pricing structure, 83
 cost of, 76n
 desired stock of, 76n
 flows, 5, 57, 80
 gains tax, 11, 15
 inflow, 3, 53, 57, 64, 66, 72
 levies on money holdings, 89
 market, 46
 market equilibrium, 2, 48, 50, 54, 59, 69, 73n
 outflow, 5, 53
 share parameter, 76n
 stock, depreciation of, 76
 supply functions, 47, 68, 69
cash-in-advance economy, 13
cash transactions, 85
central bank, 11, 22, 22n, 23, 29, 72, 93

certainty equivalence, 31, 93
Clark, 75
closed form solutions, 35
Clower, 7n
Clower constraint, 7n
Cobb-Douglas production function, 48, 68, 69, 76n
commitment, 4, 22, 89n
comparative static results, 90
comparison between exchange rate regimes 6
compensation of losers, 5
compensatory variability, 61
computers, 75n
concavity, 88, 91
consumption smoothing, 89
continuous market clearing, 6
convergence of equity yields, 53
corporate tax structure, 33
correlation
 between capital productivities, 17, 20, 30, 33
 between equity returns, 51
 between stock index returns, 8
 between stock returns and inflation, 9
cost of holding money, 85
covariance
 between productivities
 in two countries, 20n
 between returns on investment
 in two countries, 43, 73n
covered interest rate parity, 72
credit cards, 85
credit transactions, 85
critical value of wealth, 55
currency risk premium. *See* foreign exchange risk premium
current account, 89, 89n

Debreu, 8, 8n
demand functions for assets, 46
democracy, 65
depreciation deductions for corporations, 9
depreciation rates, 75n
direction of capital flows, 53
dispersion of predictable variations, 83
distributional issues, 4, 64-66, 80

diversification of wealth, 2, 62
Dooley, 58n
Dornbusch, 40n, 42n, 76n, 84, 88
Dornbusch-Frenkel model, 84, 88
Drèze, 29n
Driffill, 9n
dynamic consistency. *See* time consistency

econometric estimates of investment equation, 3, 73
effect of
  exchange rate risk, 1, 39-70, 71-82
  floating the exchange rate, 52-57, 71-82
  inflationary variability on income, 4, 83-94
  inflation risk, 1, 7-38
  monetary regime on investment, 31
  monetary regime on portfolio variance, 30, 37-38
  monetary regime on welfare, 1, 2, 4, 8, 29-34
  return uncertainty on savings, 2, 29n, 34
  unexpected inflation on stock returns, 9
  variable inflation on capital stock and consumption, 83-94
efficiency, 61-65, 80
Eichengreen, 39, 39n
electronic banking, 85
estimates of investment equations, 75-79
Ettlin, 78
Euler equations, 87n, 90n
European Monetary System, 73
European Monetary Union, 80
European Union, 64
exchange rate
  dynamics, 43n
  regime, 6, 39-70, 71-82
  risk, 2, 3, 5, 39-70, 71
  risk, and effect on capital stock, 75
  risk, free hedging of, 54
  risk, fully diversifiable, 40, 54
  risk premium. *See* foreign exchange risk premium
  stabilization, 80
  uncertainty, 73, 78n
  variability, 39, 39n, 61, 73
exchange system, 84
exogenous production, 7
expected utility, 2, 7, 29, 30, 42, 67
externality, 62, 64n

Fair, 75, 75n, 77n
Fama, 8, 9
Federal Reserve Bank of Cleveland, 83n
Feldstein, 2, 3, 9, 40, 58, 88

Feldstein-Horioka puzzle, 40, 58-59
Fischer, 29n, 76n
fixed exchange rate, 4, 5, 6, 22-38, 39-66, 71-74. *See also* regime
  potential advantage of, 5
  system, 5
  zone, 5
Fleming, 6, 6n
flexible exchange rate, 2, 3, 6, 23-38, 39-66, 71-80. *See also* regime
foreign asset position, 61n
foreign exchange risk premium, 2, 3, 40, 42, 43n, 44, 49n, 52, 54, 71, 72, 80
forward exchange
  market, 2, 42, 43n, 71
  transactions, 71
franc-dollar exchange rate, 73, 74
Frankel, 3n, 32n, 40, 49n, 54, 58n, 71n, 72, 72n
free float of the Swiss franc, 73
Frenkel, 84, 89
Friedman, 83
fully anticipated fluctuations, 1, 3
fully predictable monetary variability, 93

Gertler, 7n, 83, 84
government bonds as future tax liabilities, 49
Grandmont, 7n
Green, 2, 9, 88
Grinols, 7n, 40, 54, 83, 84
growth models with money, 87n

Hall, 32n
hedging
  cost of, 2, 42, 49, 71n, 72
  costless, 50
  of exchange rate risk, 2, 42-54, 71
  full, 44, 61n
Helpman, 6, 7, 11n, 30
Henderson, 42n
Hey, 29n
Hirshleifer, 8, 8n
home bias of investment, 3, 40, 58, 59
Horioka, 3, 40, 58
Howe, 77

income
  from money creation, 89n
  gain, 64
industrialization, 5
inflation
  risk, 1, 2, 7-38, 39, 83
  risk, measure of, 84

steadying of, 5, 93n
targeting, 61
taxation, 88
theory, 11
uncertainty, 7n, 9n, 39, 83, 83n, 84
variability, 4, 83-94
inside assets, 49
interest deduction, 33
international
   allocation of capital, 5, 40, 52
   capital market, 89
   coordination of choices, 5
   liberalization of trade, 4
   portfolio diversification, 8, 17, 29, 34, 34n, 62, 65
intertemporal
   elasticity of substitution, 32n
   optimization, 89n
inter-war period, 39n
investment
   accelerator model of, 75n
   adjustment costs of, 89
   and disinvestment, 89
   equation, 77, 78n, 79
   role of opportunities, 3-5, 48-70, 72
   q-model of, 75n
   theory, 8
   under different monetary regimes, 32
   under a fixed exchange rate, 33

Jansen, 84
Jorgenson, 76n

Kehoe, 8
Keynesian stabilization policies, 6
Kupiec, 8, 17n
Kydland, 8

labor mobility, 6
liberalization of international capital flows 40, 64
life-cycle model, 8
log utility function, 31
Lucas, 6, 7, 7n, 13, 33, 90n
Lucas critique, 90n

MacArthur, 3n, 71n, 72
MacDougall, 40, 64n
macroeconomic equilibrium, 46-51
managed floating, 39n
Mathieson, 58n
mean-variance utility function, 67
Mirman, 8

misallocation of savings, 64
Mizon, 9n
mobility of resources, 6
Modigliani, 29n
monetary
   arrangement, 4
   authority, 88, 89n
   equilibrium, 7n
   growth model, 3, 84, 84n, 87n
   policy, 2, 3, 23, 33, 34, 61, 83
   pooling, 14
   risk, 13
   system, 5, 94
   variability, 90n, 91, 92
monetary regimes, 22-29, 73
   and effect on investment and welfare, 2, 4, 29-34
   and effect on savings and investment, 7, 11
   in the post-war period, 3, 71-82
   and neutrality with respect to investment, 32
   and states of the world, 24, 26, 27, 28
   and variations in inflation, 5
money
   demand, 11, 13
   as factor of production, 84
   growth variability, 90
   market equilibrium, 14
   as non interest-bearing asset, 84n
   productivity of, 85, 86
   satiation level of, 85, 88n, 92
   "shopping services of", 84
   stock control, 34
   stock fixing, 22
   stock targeting, 1, 3, 73
   supply, 11, 13, 88
   supply variability, 4
   transfer, 13, 14
multinational firms, 7n
Mundell, 6, 6n
Mussa, 39

national identity of resource owners, 61
neoclassical theory, 76n
net foreign asset position, 40, 59-61
Niehans, 6n, 40, 43n
nominal capital gains tax, 9, 11
non-neutrality
   of tax system, 2, 9
   of returns with respect to inflation, 34, 39
numerical simulation, 35

104   Index

obstacles to international dispersion of savings, 58
OECD, 75n, 77n
   countries, 8
official restrictions on the export of capital 58
one-good assumption, 14
one-good model, 25
optimal
   exchange rate regime, 62
   international allocation of savings, 64
   level of exchange rate variance, 61-66
   monetary regime, 33-34
   portfolio, 29, 44, 45, 51
optimum currency area, 6
ordering
   of monetary regimes, 1
   of monetary regimes with respect to investment, 2, 31-33
   of monetary regimes with respect to portfolio variance, 29-30, 37-38
   of monetary regimes with respect to welfare, 2, 30-31
output lost to transactions, 85n
over-allocation of wealth, 62-65

pareto efficiency, 7n
Patinkin, 49n
payment technology, 85
perfect capital mobility, 58
permanent indebtedness, 89n
Pigott, 77
policy
   commitment, 22
   coordination, 25
   measures, 64n
   symmetry, 17
political
   coalitions, 65
   crises, 85
   economy considerations, 49, 61-65
   risk, 65
Poole, 6
pooling of monetary risk, 13
portfolio
   allocation, 1, 40-46, 49
   decisions, 42n, 83
   international diversification of, 17, 34, 34n
Pratt, 67
precautionary savings, 34
predictable
   reactions by the central bank, 88
   variations of inflation, 83, 88-94
preference
   formulation of, 32n
   for home and foreign goods, 42n
premium for hedging of currency risk. *See* foreign exchange risk premium
price level
   fixing, 33, 34
   risk, 1
   stabilization of, 11, 25
   targeting, 1
price rigidities, 34
productive services of money, 84-94
productivity
   gains, 64
   shocks, 48
public investment, 11
purchasing power parity, 1, 2, 8, 14, 49n
   deviations from, 34, 39

quantity theory of money, 11, 13, 14

raw material prices, 17
Razin, 6, 7, 11n, 30
reciprocal bond supplies and demands, 50
regime
   of exchange rate fixing, 1, 2, 23-38
   of flexible exchange rates, 2, 40, 73
   of money stock fixing, 1, 2, 22-38
   of one-sided exchange rate peg, 1, 2, 23-38
   of pegged currencies, 2
   of price level fixing, 1, 2, 25-38
   switch, 62n, 73, 80
   of two-sided exchange rate peg, 1, 2, 25-38
   uncertainty, 22
   volatility, 65
Reiss, 75
residency of resource owners, 64
return equalization, 51
risk aversion, 1, 3, 7n, 39, 40, 51
   constant relative, 29, 31
   degree of, 53, 66
   Pratt measure of, 67
   relative and absolute, 29
   relative, parameter of, 31, 32, 32n, 44, 46n, 67
risk neutrality, 7n, 31, 40
risk pooling, 33
risk premium. *See* foreign exchange risk premium
Ruoss, 78

Index 105

Samuelson, 90
Sandmo, 31, 35
schemes
    for distributing welfare gains, 66
    for international transfers, 64
Schwert, 9
Seldon, 32n
Sheshinski, 2, 9, 88
Sidrauski, 87n
stabilization policies, 4
state preference framework, 8
steadiness equivalence, 93
Stein, 87n
stochastic fluctuations of productivity, 11
Stockman, 13
Svensson, 8n, 13
Sweeney, 83, 84
Swiss National Bank, 3, 73
switch to flexible exchange rates, 78

tax
    liability, 49n
    on nominal capital gains, 33
    revenues, use of, 11
    structure with interest deduction, 9
    theory framework, 9
Taylor, 76n
technology
    changes in, 73n
    energy-intensive, 75n
Tesar, 58n
time consistency, 22, 89n
Tobin, 9, 9n, 88
trade-off between return and risk, 51
transaction periods, 14n
transfer payments, 5, 64, 80, 84, 87
transfer scheme, 5
transition
    to fixed exchange rates, 5
    to flexible exchange rates, 2, 3, 61, 71-80. *See also* effect of floating the exchange rate
transnational structure, 64
Turnovsky, 40, 54
two-country
    model, 34, 40, 66
    world, 2, 62
two-period
    frame, 8
    version, 13

Ulph, 9n
unemployment, 6, 34
utility function,
    additive, 32n

quadratic, 29, 32, 35, 42, 67
von Neuman-Morgenstern, 42
with constant relative risk aversion, 31

velocity of circulation, 11

Wang, 88n
wealth threshold, 56
welfare, 1, 8, 34, 61, 66
    differences between regimes, 30
    gains, 4
    improving transfer payments, 65
    ordering, 30
world
    capital stock, 3, 58
    interest rate, 89
    output, 63

Yip, 88n
Younes, 7n

Berner Beiträge zur Nationalökonomie

Dr. Sylvia Kaufmann

Permanente Komponenten makroökonomischer Variablen

«Berner Beiträge zur Nationalökonomie» Band 69
97 Seiten, 10 Abbildungen, 19 Tabellen
kartoniert Fr. 28.– / DM 31.– / öS 242.–
ISBN 3-258-05040-6

Die «Real Business Cycles»-Theorie vertritt die Ansicht, dass kurzfristige Schwankungen, die sogenannten Konjunkturschwankungen, durch Schocks in den Wachstumskomponenten makroökonomischer Zeitreihen verursacht werden und als Anpassungsmechanismen an den neuen Gleichgewichtswachstumspfad zu interpretieren sind. Die Untersuchung schätzt mit Hilfe neuerer ökonometrischer Verfahren die Wichtigkeit solcher permanenten Komponenten in sechs Schweizer Makrovariablen.

Haupt

Berner Beiträge zur Nationalökonomie

Dr. Hansjörg Borutta

Integrierte Prozesse und gemeinsame Trends

Darstellung und empirische Umsetzung mit Hilfe von Vektorfehlerkorrekturmodellen und Bayesianischen Vektorautoregressionen

«Berner Beiträge zur Nationalökonomie» Band 68
X + 227 Seiten, 15 Abbildungen, 67 Tabellen
kartoniert Fr. 44.– / DM 49.– / öS 382.–
ISBN 3-258-05018-X

Die Idee, Wirtschaftsdaten als nicht-stationäre Prozesse zu begreifen, die jedoch von gemeinsamen Trends getrieben werden und sich deshalb nicht beliebig voneinander entfernen können, beflügelt Ökonomen und Statistiker gleichermassen. Folglich sind integrierte Prozesse, Kointegration und gemeinsame Trends innerhalb weniger Jahre zum festen Bestandteil der modernen Ökonometrie geworden. Der Autor beschäftigt sich mit der Frage, welchen praktischen, sprich prognostischen Nutzen diese Konzepte haben und stellt einen Vergleich mit der weniger populären Bayesianischen Vektorautoregression an. Die theoretischen Abhandlungen werden durch ausführliche empirische Anwendungen ergänzt.

Haupt

Berner Beiträge zur Nationalökonomie

Dr. Thomas Jordan

Seigniorage, Defizite, Verschuldung und Europäische Währungsunion

«Berner Beiträge zur Nationalökonomie» Band 67
XV + 342 Seiten, 15 Grafiken, 44 Tabellen
kartoniert Fr. 54.– / DM 60.– / öS 468.–
ISBN 3-258-04897-5

Das Buch untersucht die realwirtschaftlichen und monetären Konsequenzen für die Europäische Union als ganzes, die bei der Bildung einer Europäischen Währungsunion aus dem Verlust der nationalen geldpolitischen Autonomie der Teilnehmerstaaten und folglich aus dem Verlust der Bestimmungen der Höhe der nationalen Seigniorageeinnahmen (Einnahmen aus Geldschöpfung) entstehen können.

Haupt

Berner Beiträge zur Nationalökonomie

Dr. Urs Graf

Geldpolitische Aspekte finanzieller Innovationen

Eine Analyse mikro- und makroökonomischer Implikationen

«Berner Beiträge zur Nationalökonomie» Band 66
VI + 225 Seiten, 14 Abbildungen, 4 Tabellen
kartoniert Fr. 44.– / DM 49.– / öS 382.–
ISBN 3-258-04894-0

Das Buch befasst sich mit den Konsequenzen von finanziellen Innovationen, d.h. von Neuerungen auf Geld-, Kredit- und Kapitalmärkten, für die Geldpolitik aus theoretischer Sicht. Es setzt sich mit den Auswirkungen von Finanzinnovationen und regulatorischen Änderungen auf die Geldnachfrage und auf die Reservennachfrage der Banken aus mikroökonomischer Sicht auseinander. Weiter werden Makromodelle mit rationalen Erwartungen diskutiert und insbesondere Fragen der monetären Kontrolle und des Einsatzes der geldpolitischen Instrumente untersucht.

Haupt